The Inn at the Red Oak

THE INN AT THE RED OAK

"It's a treasure right enough!" cried Dan.

THE INN AT THE RED OAK

BY
LATTA GRISWOLD

M

L.C.

ROBERT J. SHORES
NEW YORK

Copyright, 1917, by
ROBERT J. SHORES, Publisher
New York

CONTENTS

THE OLD MARQUIS
PART I

PART II
THE TORN SCRAP OF PAPER

PART III
THE SCHOONER IN THE COVE

PART IV
THE ATTACK ON THE INN

The Inn at the Red Oak

PART I

THE OLD MARQUIS

CHAPTER I

THE MARQUIS ARRIVES AT THE INN

By the end of the second decade of the last century Monday Port had passed the height of prosperity as one of the principal depots for the West Indian trade. The shipping was rapidly being transferred to New York and Boston, and the old families of the Port, having made their fortunes, in rum and tobacco as often as not, were either moving away to follow the trade or had acquiesced in the changed conditions and were settling down to enjoy the fruit of their labours. The harbour now was frequently deserted, except for an occasional coastwise trader; the streets began to wear that melancholy aspect of a town whose good days are more a memory

than a present reality; and the old stage roads
to Coventry and Perth Anhault were no longer
the arteries of travel they once had been.

To the east of Monday Port, across Deal Great
Water, an estuary of the sea that expanded almost to the dignity of a lake, lay a pleasant roll-
ing wooded country known in Caesarea as Deal.
It boasted no village, scarcely a hamlet.   Dr.
Jeremiah Watson, a famous pedagogue and a
graduate of Kingsbridge, had started his modest
establishment for "the education of the sons of
gentlemen" on Deal Hill; there were half-a-
dozen prospering farms, Squire Pembroke's Red
Farm and Judge Meath's curiously lonely but
beautiful House on the Dunes among them; a
little Episcopalian chapel on the shores of the
Strathsey river, a group of houses at the cross
roads north of Lovel's Woods, and the Inn at the
Red Oak,—and that was all.

In its day this inn had been a famous hostelry,
much more popular with travellers than the ill-
kept provincial hotels in Monday Port; but now
for a long time it had scarcely provided a liveli-
hood for old Mrs. Frost, widow of the famous
Peter who for so many years had been its popular
host.   No one knew when the house had been

built; though there was an old corner stone on which local antiquarians professed to decipher the figures "1693," and that year was assigned by tradition as the date of its foundation.

It was a long crazy building, with a great sloping roof, a wide porch running its entire length, and attached to its sides and rear in all sorts of unexpected ways and places were numerous out houses and offices. Behind its high brick chimneys rose the thick growth of Lovel's Woods, crowning the ridge that ran between Beaver Pond and the Strathsey river to the sea. The house faced southwards, and from the cobbled court before it meadow and woodland sloped to the beaches and the long line of sand dunes that straggled out and lost themselves in Strathsey Neck. To the east lay marshes and the dunes and beyond them the Strathsey, two miles wide where its waters met those of the Atlantic; west lay the great curve, known as the Second Beach, the blue surface of Deal Bay, and a line of rocky shore, three miles in length, terminated by Rough Point, near which began the out-lying houses of Monday Port.

The old hostelry took its name from a giant oak which grew at its doorstep just to one side of the maple-lined driveway that led down to the Port Road, a hundred yards or so beyond. This enormous tree spread its branches over the entire width and half the length of the roof. Ordinarily, of course, its foliage was as green as the leaves on the maples of the avenue or on the neighbouring elms, and the name of the Inn might have seemed to the summer or winter traveller an odd misnomer; but in autumn when the frost came early and the great mass of green flushed to a deep crimson it could not have been known more appropriately than as the Inn at the Red Oak.

It was a solidly-built house, such as even in the early part of the nineteenth century men were complaining they could no longer obtain; built to weather centuries of biting southeasters, and—the legend ran—to afford protection in its early days against Indians. At the time of the Revolution it had been barricaded, pierced with portholes, and had served, like innumerable other houses from Virginia to Massachusetts, as Washington's headquarters. When Tom Pembroke knew it best, its old age and decay had well set in.

Pembroke was the son of the neighbouring squire, whose house, known as the Red Farm, lay in the little valley on the other side of the Woods at the head of Beaver Pond. From the time he had been able to thread his way across the woodland by its devious paths—Tom had been at the Inn almost every day to play with Dan Frost, the landlord's son. · They had played in the stables, then stocked with a score of horses, where now there were only two or three; in the great hay-mows of the old barn in the clearing back of the Inn; in the ramshackle garret under that amazing roof; or, best of all, in the abandoned bowling-alley, where they rolled delapidated balls at rickety ten-pins.

When Tom and Dan were eighteen—they were born within a day of each other one bitter February—old Peter died, leaving the Inn to his wife. Mrs. Frost pretended to carry on the business, but the actual task of doing so soon devolved upon her son. And in this he was subjected to little interference; for the poor lady, kindly inefficient soul that she was, became almost helpless with rheumatism. But indeed it was rather on the farm than to the Inn that more and more they depended for their living. In the social hierarchy of Caesarea the Pembrokes held themselves as vastly superior to the Frosts; but thanks to the easy-going democratic customs of the young republic, more was made of this by the women than the men.

The two boys loved each other devotedly, though love is doubtless the last word they would have chosen to express their relation. Dan was tall, dark, muscular; he had a well-shaped head on his square shoulders; strong well-cut features; a face that the sun had deeply tanned and dark hair that it had burnished with gold. Altogether he was a prepossessing lad, though he looked several years older than he was, and he was commonly treated by his neighbours with a consideration that his years did not merit. Tom Pembroke was fairer; more attractive, perhaps, on first acquaintance; certainly more boyish in appearance and behaviour. He was quicker in his movements and in his mental processes; more aristocratic in his bearing. His blue eyes were more intelligent than Dan's, but no less frank and kindly. Young Frost admired his friend almost as much as he cared for him; for Dan, deprived of schooling, had a reverence for learning, of which Tom had got a smattering at Dr. Watson's establishment for "the sons of gentlemen" on the nearby hill.

One stormy night in early January, the eve of Dan Frosts's twenty-second birthday, the two young men had their supper together at the Inn, and afterwards sat for half-an-hour in the hot, stove-heated parlour until Mrs. Frost began to nod over her knitting.

"Off with you, boys," she said at length; "you will be wanting to smoke your dreadful pipes. Nancy will keep me company."

They took instant advantage of this permission and went into the deserted bar, where they made a roaring fire on the great hearth, drew their chairs near, filled their long clay pipes with Virginia tobacco, and fell to talking.

"Think of it!" exclaimed young Frost, as he took a great whiff at his pipe; "here we are—the middle of the winter—and not a guest in the house. Why we used to have a dozen travellers round the bar here, and the whole house bustling. I've known my father to serve a hundred and more with rum on a night like this. Now we do a fine business if we serve as many in a winter. Times have changed since we were boys."

"Aye," Tom agreed, "and it isn't so long ago, either. It seemed to me as if the whole county used to be here on a Saturday night."

"I'm thinking," resumed Dan musingly, "of throwing up the business, what's the use of pretending to keep an inn? If it wasn't for mother and for Nancy, I'd clear out, boy; go off and hunt my fortune. As it is, with what I make on the farm and lose on the house, I just pull through the year."

"By gad," exclaimed Tom, "I'd go with you, Dan. I'm tired to my soul with reading law in father's office. Why, you and I haven't been farther than Coventry to the county fair, or to Perth Anhault to make a horse trade. I'd like to see the world, go to London and Paris. I've wanted to go to France ever since that queer Frenchman was here—remember?—and told us those jolly tales about the Revolution and the great Napoleon. We were hardly more than seven or eight then, I guess."

"I would like to go, hanged if I wouldn't," said Dan. "I'm getting more and more discontented. But there's not much use crying for the moon, and France might as well be the moon, for all of me." He relapsed then into a brooding silence. It was hard for an inn-keeper to be cheerful in mid-winter with an empty house. Tom too was silent, dreaming vividly, if vaguely, of the France he longed to see.

"Hark!" exclaimed Dan presently. "How it

blows! There must be a big sea outside to-night."

He strode to the window, pushed back the curtains of faded chintz, and stared out into the darkness. The wind was howling in the trees and
about the eaves of the old inn, the harsh roar of
the surf mingled with the noise of the storm, and
the sleet lashed the window-panes in fury.

"You will not be thinking of going home to-
night, Tom?"

"Not I," Pembroke answered, for he was as
much at home in Dan's enormous chamber as he
was in his own little room under the roof at the
Red Farm.

As he turned from the window, the door into the
parlour opened, and a young girl quietly slipped
in and seated herself in the chimney-corner.

"Hello, Nance," Dan exclaimed, as she entered;
"come close, child; you need to be near the fire on
a night like this."

"Mother is asleep," the girl answered briefly,
and then, resting her chin upon her hands, she
fixed her great dark eyes upon the glowing logs.
She was Dan's foster-sister, eighteen years of age,
though she looked hardly more than sixteen; a
shy, slender, girl, lovely with a wild, unusual
charm. To Tom she had always been a silent

elfin creature, delightful as their playmate when a child, but now though still so familiar, she seemed in an odd way, to grow more remote. Apparently she liked to sit with them on these winter evenings in the deserted bar, when Mrs. Frost had gone to bed; and to listen to their conversation, though she took little part in it.

As Dan resumed his seat, he looked at her with evident concern, for she was shivering as she sat so quietly by the fireside.

"Are you cold, Nance?" he asked.

"A little," she replied. "I was afraid in the parlour with Mother asleep, and the wind and the waves roaring so horribly."

"Afraid?" exclaimed Tom, with an incredulous laugh. "I never knew you to be really afraid of anything in the world, Nancy."

She turned her dark eyes upon him for the moment, with a sharp inquisitive glance which caused him to flush unaccountably. An answering crimson showed in her cheeks, and she turned back to the fire. The colour fled almost as quickly as it had come, and left her pale, despite the glow of firelight.

"I was afraid—to-night," she said, after a moment's silence.

Suddenly there came the sound of a tremendous knocking on the door which opened from the bar into the outer porch, and all three started in momentary alarm.

Dan jumped to his feet. "Who's that?" he cried.

Again came the vigorous knocking. He ran across the room, let down the great oaken beam, and opened the door to the night and storm.

"Come in, travellers." A gust of wind and sleet rushed through the opening and stung their faces. With the gust there seemed to blow in the figure of a little old man wrapped in a great black coat, bouncing into their midst as if he were an India rubber ball thrown by a gigantic hand. Behind him strode in Manners, the liveryman of Monday Port.

"Here's a guest for you, Mr. Frost. I confess I did my best to keep him in town till morning, but nothing 'd do; he must get to the Inn at the Red Oak to-night. We had a hellish time getting here too, begging the lady's pardon; but here we are."

Good-naturedly he had taken hold of his fare and, as he spoke, was helping the stranger unwrap himself from the enveloping cloak.

"He's welcome," said Dan. "Here, sir, let me

help you." He put out his hand to steady the curious old gentleman, who, at last, gasping for breath and blinking the sleet out of his eyes, had been unrolled by Manners from the dripping cloak.

He was a strange figure of a man, they thought, as Dan led him to the fire to thaw himself out. He was scarcely more than five and a half feet in height, with tiny hands and feet almost out of proportion even to his diminutive size. He was an old man, they would have said, though his movements were quick and agile as if he were set up on springs. His face, small, sharp-featured and weazened, was seamed with a thousand wrinkles. His wig was awry, its powder, washed out by the melting sleet, was dripping on his face in pasty streaks; and from beneath it had fallen wisps of thin grey hair, which plastered themselves against his temples and forehead. This last feature was also out of proportion to the rest of his physigonomy, for it was of extraordinary height, and of a polished smoothness, in strange contrast to his wrinkled cheeks. Beneath shone two flashing black eyes, with the fire of youth in them, for all he seemed so old. The lower part of his face was less distinctive. He had a small, sharply-pointed nose; a weak mouth, half-hidden by drooping white moustaches; and a small sharp chin, accentuated by a white beard nattily trimmed to a point. He was dressed entirely in black; a flowing coat of French cut, black small clothes, black stockings and boots that reached to the calves of his little legs. These boots were ornamented with great silver buckles, and about his neck and wrists showed bedraggled bits of yellowed lace.

He stood before the fire, speechless still; standing first on one foot then on the other; rubbing his hands the while as he held them to the grateful warmth.

Nancy had in the meanwhile drawn a glass of rum, and now advancing held it toward him a little gingerly. He took it eagerly and drained it at a gulp.

"*Merci, ma petite ange; merci, messieurs,*" he exclaimed at last; and then added in distinct, though somewhat strongly accented English, "I ask your pardon. I forget you may not know my language. But now that this good liquor has put new life in my poor old bones, I explain myself. I am arrived, I infer, at the Inn at the Red Oak; and you, monsieur, though so young, I take to be my host. I have your description, you perceive, from the good postilion. You will do me the kindness to provide me with supper and a bed?"

"Certainly, sir," said Dan. "It is late and we are unprepared, but we will put you up somehow. You too, Manners, had best let me bunk you till morning; you'll not be going back to the Port tonight? Nancy a fresh bumper for Mr. Manners."

"Thankee, sir; I managed to get out with the gentleman yonder, and I guess I'll manage to get back. But it's a rare night, masters. Just a minute, sir, and I'll be getting his honour's bags... Thank ye kindly, Miss Nancy."

He drained the tumbler of raw spirit that Nancy held out. Then he opened the door again and went out into the storm, returning almost at once with the stranger's bags.

Dan turned to his sister. "Nancy dear, go stir up Susan and Deborah. We must have a fire made in the south chamber and some hot supper got ready. Tell Susan to rout out Jesse to help her. Say nothing to Mother; no need to disturb her. And now, sir," he continued, turning again to the stranger, "may I ask your name?"

The old gentleman ceased his springing seesaw

for a moment, and fixed his keen black eyes on the
questioner.

"*Certainment, monsieur*—certainly, I should
say," he replied in a high, but not unpleasant,
voice. "I am the Marquis de Boisdhyver, at your
service. I am to travel in the United States—oh!
for a long time. I stay here, if you are so good as
to accommodate me, perhaps till you are weary
and wish me to go elsewhere. You have been
greatly recommended to me by my friend,—quiet,
remote, secluded, an *auberge*—what you call it?—
an inn, well-suited to my habits, my tastes, my desire for rest. I am very *fatigué*, monsieur."

"Yes," said Dan, with a grim smile, "we are remote and quiet and secluded. You are welcome,
sir, to what we have. Tom, see that Manners has
another drink before he goes, will you? and do the
honours for our guest, while Nance and I get
things ready."

As he disappeared into the kitchen, following
Nancy, the Marquis looking after him with a com-
ical expression of gratitude upon his face. Tom
drew another glass of rum, which Manners eagerly, if rashly, devoured. Then the liveryman
wrapped himself in his furs, bade them good-night,

and started out again into the storm for his drive back to Monday Port.

All this time the old gentleman stood warming his feet and hands at the fire, watching his two companions with quickly-shifting eyes, or glancing curiously over the great bar which the light of the fire and the few candles but faintly illuminated.

Having barred the door, Tom turned back to the hearth. "It is a bad night, sir."

"But yes," exclaimed the Marquis. "I think I perish. Oh! that dreary tavern at your Monday Port. I think when I arrive there I prefer to perish. But this, this is the old Inn at the Red Oak, is it not? And it dates, yes,—from the year 1693? The old inn, eh, by the great tree?"

"Yes, certainly," Pembroke answered; "at least, that is the date that some people claim is on the old cornerstone. You have been here before then, sir?"

"I?" exclaimed Monsieur de Boisdhyver. "Oh, no! not I. I have heard from my friend who was here some years ago."

"Oh, I see. And you have come far to-day?"

"From Coventry, monsieur—Monsieur—?"

"Pembroke," Tom replied, with a little start.

"Ah! yes, Monsieur Pembroke. A member of the household?"

"No—a friend."

"I make a mistake," quickly interposed the traveller, "Pardon. I am come from Coventry, Monsieur Pembroke, in an everlasting an eternal stage, a monster of a carriage, monsieur. It is only a few days since that I arrive from France."

"Ah, France!" exclaimed Tom, recalling that only a little while before he and Dan had been dreaming of that magic country. And here was a person who actually lived in France, who had just come from there, who extraordinarily chose to leave that delightful land for the Inn at the Red Oak in mid-winter.

"France," he repeated; "all my life, sir, I have been longing to go there."

"So?" said the Marquis, raising his white eyebrows with interest. "You love *ma belle patrie,* eh? *Qui Sait?*—you will perhaps some day go there. You have interests, friends in my country?"

"No, none," Tom answered. "I wish I had. You come from Paris, sir?"

"*Mais oui.*"

For some time they chatted in such fashion, the Marquis answering Tom's many questions with characteristic French politeness, but turning ever and anon a pathetic glance toward the door through which Dan and Nancy had disappeared. It was with undisguised satisfaction that he greeted young Frost when he returned to announce that supper was ready.

"I famish!" the old gentleman exclaimed. "I have dined to-day on a biscuit and a glass of water."

They found the kitchen table amply spread with food, — cold meats, hot eggs and coffee, and a bottle of port. Monsieur de Boisdhyver ate heartily and drank his wine with relish, gracefully toasting Nancy as he did so. When his meal was finished, he begged with many excuses to be shown to his bedroom; and indeed his fatigue was evident. Dan saw him to the great south chamber, carrying a pair of lighted candles before. He made sure that all had been done that sulky sleepy maids could be induced to do, and then left him to make ready for the night.

Lights were extinguished in the parlour and the bar, the fires were banked, and the two young men went up to Dan's own room. There on either side of the warm hearth, had been drawn two great four-posted beds, and it took the lads but a moment to tumble into them.

"It's queer," said Dan, as he pulled the comfort snugly about his shoulders, calling to Tom across the way; "it's queer—the old chap evidently means to stay awhile. What does a French marquis want in a deserted hole like this, I'd like to know? But if he pays, why the longer he stays the better."

"I hope he does," said Tom sleepily. "He has a reason, I fancy, for he asked questions enough while you were out seeing to his supper. He seems to know the place almost as well as if he had been here before, though he said he hadn't. But, by gad, I wish you and I were snug in a little hotel on the banks of the Seine to-night and not bothering our heads about a doddering old marquis who hadn't sense enough to stay there."

"Wish we were," Dan replied. "Good-night," he called, realizing that his friend was too sleepy to lie awake and discuss any longer their unexpected guest.

"Good-night," murmured Tom, and promptly drifted away into dreams of the wonderful land he had never seen. As for Dan he lay awake a long time, wondering what could possibly have brought the old Marquis to the deserted inn at such a time of the year and on such a night.

CHAPTER II

Toward daylight the storm blew itself out, the wind swung round to the northwest, and the morning dawned clear and cold, with a sharp breeze blowing and a bright sun shining upon a snow-clad, ice-crusted world and a sparkling sapphire sea.

Dan had risen early and had set Jesse to clear a way across the court and down the avenue to the road. The maids, astir by dawn, were no longer sulky but bustled about at the preparation of an unusually good breakfast in honour of the new guest.

Mrs. Frost, who habitually lay till nine or ten o'clock behind the crimson curtains of her great bed, had caught wind of something out of the ordinary, demanded Nancy's early assistance, and announced her intention of breakfasting with the household.

She was fretful during the complicated process of her toilette and so hurt the feelings of her

20

foster-daughter, that when Dan came to take her into the breakfast room, Nancy found an excuse for not accompanying them.

The Marquis was awaiting their appearance. He stood with his back to the fire, a spruce and carefully-dressed little figure, passing remarks upon the weather with young Pembroke, who leaned his graceful length against the mantelpiece.

The noble traveller was presented with due ceremony to Mrs. Frost, who greeted him with old-world courtesy. She had had, indeed, considerably more association with distinguished personages than had most of the dames of the neighbouring farms who considered themselves her social superiors. She welcomed Monsieur de Boisdhyver graciously, enquiring with interest of his journey and with solicitude as to his rest during the night. She received with satisfaction his rapturous compliments on the comforts that had been provided him, on the beauty of the surrounding country upon which he had looked from the windows of his chamber, and on her own condescension in vouchsafing to breakfast with them. She was delighted that he should find the Inn at the Red Oak so much to his taste that he proposed to stay with them indefinitely.

They' were soon seated at the breakfast-table and had addressed themselves to the various good things that black Deborah had provided. The native Johnny cakes, made of meal ground by their own windmill, the Marquis professed to find particularly tempting.

Despite Mrs. Frost's questions, despite his own voluble replies, Monsieur de Boisdhyver gave no hint, that there was any deeper reason for his seeking exile at the Inn of the Red Oak than that he desired rest and quiet and had been assured that he would find them there. And who had so complimented their simple abode of hospitality ?

"Ah, madame," he murmered, lifting his tiny hands, "so many !"

"But I fear, monsieur," replied his hostess, "that you, who are accustomed to the luxuries of a splendid city like Paris, to so many things of which we read, will find little to interest and amuse you in our remote countryside."

"As for interest, madame," the Marquis protested, "there are the beauties of nature, your so delightful household, my few books, my writing; and for amusement, I have my violin;—I so love to play. You will not mind ?—perhaps, enjoy it ?"

"Indeed yes," said Mrs. Frost. "Dan, too, is a fiddler after a fashion; and as for Nancy, she has a passion for music, and dreams away many an evening while my son plays his old tunes."

"Ah, yes," said the Marquis, "Mademoiselle Nancy, I have not the pleasure to see her this morning ?"

"No," replied Mrs. Frost, flushing a trifle at the recollection of why Nancy was not present, "she is somewhat indisposed—a mere trifle. You will see her later in the day. But, monsieur, you should have come to us in the spring or the summer, for then the country is truly beautiful; now, with these snow-bound roads, when not even the stage-coach passes, we are indeed lonely and remote."

"It is that," insisted the Marquis, "which so charms me. When one is old and when one has lived a life too occupied, it is this peace, this quiet, this remoteness one desires. To walk a little, to sit by your so marvellously warm fires, to look upon your beautiful country, *cest bou !*"

He held her for a moment with his piercing little eyes, a faint smile upon his lips, as though to say that it was impossible he should be con- vinced that he had not found precisely what he was seeking, and insisting, as it were, that his hostess take his words as the compliment they were designed to be.

Before she had time to reply, he had turned to Dan. "What a fine harbour you have, Monsieur Frost," he said, pointing through the window toward the Cove, seperated from the river and the sea by the great curve of Strathsey Neck, its blue waters sparkling now in the light of the morning sun.

"Yes," replied Dan, glancing out upon the well-known shoreline, "it is a good harbour, though nothing, of course, to compare with a Port. But it's seldom that we see a ship at anchor here, now."

"There is, however," inquired the Marquis with interest, "anchorage for a vessel, a large vessel?"

"Yes, indeed," Tom interrupted, "in the old days when my father had his ships plying between Havana and the Port, he would often have them anchor in the Cove for convenience in lading them with corn from the farm."

"And they were large ships?"

"Full-rigged, sir; many of 'em, and drawing eight feet at least."

"*Eh bien !* And the old Inn, madame, it dates, your son tells me, from 1693 ?"

"We think so, sir, though I have no positive

knowledge of its existence before 1750. My husband purchased the place in '94, and it had then been a hostelry for some years, certainly from the middle of the century. But we have made many additions. Danny dear, perhaps it will interest the Marquis if you should take him over the house. We are proud of our old inn, sir."

"And with reason, madame. If monsieur will, I shall be charmed."

"I will leave you then with my son. Give me your arm, Dan, to the parlour. Unfortunately, Monsieur le Marquis, affliction has crippled me and I spend the day in my chair in the blue parlour. I shall be so pleased, if you will come and chat with me. Tommy, you will be staying to dinner with us ?"

"Thank you, Mrs. Frost, but I must get to the Port for the day. Mother and Father are leaving by the afternoon stage, if it gets through. They are going to spend the winter in Coventry. But I shall be back to-night as I have promised Dan to spend that time with him."

"We shall be glad to have you, as you know."

Soon after Mrs. Frost had left the breakfast-room and Tom had started forth with horse and sleigh, Dan returned. The Marquis promptly

reminded him of the suggestion that he should
be taken over the Inn. It seemed to Dan an
uninteresting way to entertain his guest and the
morning was a busy one. However, he promised
to be ready at eleven o'clock to show the Marquis
all there was in the old house.

As Dan went about the offices and stables, per-
forming himself much of the work that in pros-
perous times fell to grooms and hostlers, he found
himself thinking about his new guest. Dan knew
enough of French history to be aware there were
frequent occasions in France when partisans of the
various factions, royalist, imperialist, or repub-
lican, found it best to expatriate themselves. He
knew that in times past many of the most distinguished exiles had found asylum in America.
But at the present, he understood, King Louis
Philippe, was reigning quietly at the Tuileries and,
moreover, the Marquis de Boisdhyver, mysterious
as he was, did not suggest the political adventurer
of whom Dan as a boy had heard his parents tell
such extraordinary tales. In the few years immediately after the final fall of the great Bonaparte there had been an influx of imperialistic
supporters in America, some of whom had even
found their way to Monday Port and Deal. One

of these, Dan remembered, had stayed for some months in '14 or '15 at the Inn at the Red Oak, and it was he whom Tom had recalled the night before as having told them stories of his adventurous exploits in the wars of the Little Corporal. But it was too long after Napoleon's fall to connect his present guest with the imperial exiles. He could imagine no ulterior reason for the Marquis's coming and was inclined to put it down as the caprice of an old restless gentleman who had a genuine mania for solitude. Of solitude, certainly, he was apt to get his fill at the Inn at the Red Oak.

At eleven o'clock he returned to keep his appointment. He found the Marquis established at a small table in the bar by an east window, from which was obtained a view of the Cove, of the sand-dunes along the Neck, and of the open sea beyond. A writing-desk was on the table, ink and quills had been provided, a number of books and papers were strewn about, and Monsieur de Boisdhyver was apparently busy with his correspondence.

"Enchanted" he exclaimed, as he pulled out a great gold watch. "Punctual. I find another virtue, monsieur, in a character to which I have already had so much reason to pay my compliments. I trust I do not trespass upon your more important duties." As he spoke, he rapidly swept the papers into the writing-desk, closed and locked it, and carefully placed the tiny golden key into the pocket of his gayly-embroidered waistcoat.

"Not at all," Dan replied courteously, "I shall be glad to show you about. But I fear you will find it cold and dismal, for the greater part of the house is seldom used or even entered."

"I bring my cloak," said the Marquis. "Interest will give me warmth. What I have already seen of the Inn at the Red Oak is so charming, that I doubt not there is much more to delight one. I imagine, monsieur, how gay must have been this place once."

He took his great cloak from the peg near the fire where it had been hung the night before to dry wrapped himself snugly in it; and then, with a little bow, preceded Dan into the cold and draughty corridor that opened from the bar into the older part of the house.

This hallway extended fifty or sixty feet to the north wall of the main part of the inn whence a large window at the turn of a flight of stairs gave light. On the right, extending the same distance

as the hall itself, was a great room known as the
Red Drawing-room, into which Dan first showed
the Marquis. This room had not been used since
father's death four or five years before, and for a
long time previous to that only on the rare occasions when a county gathering of some sort
was held at the inn. It had been furnished in
good taste and style in colonial days, but was
now dilapidated and musty. The heavy red
damask curtains were drawn before the windows,
and the room was dark and cheerless. Dan admitted the dazzling light of the sun; but the
Marquis only shivered and seemed anxious to pass
quickly on.

"You see, sir," observed the young landlord,
"it is dismal enough."

"*Mais oui—mais oui*," exclaimed the Marquis.

At the foot of the stairway the corridor turned
at right angles and ran north. On either side
opened a number of chambers in like conditions of
disrepair, which had been used as bedrooms in the
palmy days of the hostelry. This corridor ended
at the bowling-alley, where as children Tom and
Dan had loved to play. Half-way to the entrance
to the bowling-alley a third hallway branched off
to the right, leading to a similar set of chambers.

Into all these they entered, the Marquis examining each with quick glances, dismissing them with the briefest interest and the most obvious comment.

Dan saved the *piéce-de-resistance* till last. This was a little room entered from the second corridor just at the turn—the only room indeed, as he truthfully said, that merited a visit.

"This," he explained, "we call the Oak Parlour. It is the only room on this floor worth showing you. My father brought the wainscoting from an old English country-house in Dorsetshire. My father's people were Torries, sir, and kept up their connection with the old country."

It was a delightful room into which Dan now admitted the light of day, drawing aside the heavy green curtains from the eastern windows. It was wainscoted from floor to cornice in old black English oak, curiously and elaborately carved, and divided into long narrow panels. The ceiling, of similar materials and alike elaborately decorated, was supported by heavy transverse beams that seemed solid and strong enough to support the roof of a cathedral. On one side two windows opened upon the gallery and court and looked out upon the Cove, on the other side stood a cabinet. It was the most striking piece of furniture in the room, of enormous dimensions and beautifully carved on the doors of the cupboards below and on the top-pieces between the mirrors were lion's heads of almost life-size. Opposite the heavy door, by which they had entered, was a large fireplace, containing a pair of elaborately ornamented brass and irons. There was not otherwise a great deal of furniture,—two or three tables, some chairs, a deep window-seat, a writing-desk of French design; but all, except this last, in keeping with the character of the room, and all brought across the seas from the old Dorsetshire mansion, from which Peter Frost had obtained the interior.

"Charmant !" exclaimed the Marquis. "You have a jewel, *mon ami;* a bit of old England or of old France in the heart of America; a room one finds not elsewhere in the States. It is a *creation superbe."*

With enthusiastic interest he moved about, touching each article of furniture, examining with care the two of three old English landscapes that had been let into panels on the west side of the room, pausing in ecstacies before the great cabinet and standing before the fireplace as if he were warming his hands at that generous hearth.

"Ah, Monsieur Frost, could I but write, read, dream here...... !"

"I fear that would be impossible, sir," replied Dan. "It is difficult to heat this portion of the house; and in fact, we never use it."

"*Hélas !*" exclaimed the Marquis, "those things which allure us in this world are so often impossible. Perhaps in the spring, in the summer, when there is no longer the necessity of the fire, you will permit me."

"It may be, monsieur," Dan replied, "that long before the summer comes you will have left us."

"*Mais non !*" cried M. de Boisdhyver. "Every hour that I stay but proves to me how long you will have to endure my company."

Somewhat ungraciously, it seemed, young Frost made no reply to this pleasantry; for already he was impatient to be gone. Although the room was intensely cold and uncomfortable, still his guest lingered, standing before the massive cabinet, exclaiming upon the exquisiteness of the workmanship, and every now and then running his dainty fingers along the carving of its front. As Dan stood waiting for the Marquis to leave, he chanced to glance through the window to the court without, and saw Jesse starting out in the sleigh. As he had given him no such order he ran quickly to the window, rapped vigourously and then, excusing himself to the Marquis, hurried out to ask Jesse to explain his errand.

The Marquis de Boisdhyver stood for a moment, as Dan left him, motionless in front of the cabinet. His face was bright with surprise and delight, his eyes alert with interest and cunning. After a moment's hesitation he stole cautiously to the window, and seeing Frost was engaged in conversation with Jesse, he sprang back with quick steps to the cabinet. He hastily ran the tips of his fingers along the beveled edges of the wide shelf from end to end several times, each time the expression of alertness deepening into one of disappointment. He stopped for a moment and listened. All was quiet. Again with quick motions he felt beneath the edges. Suddenly his eyes brightened and he breathed quickly; his sensitive fingers had detected a slight unevenness in the smooth woodwork. Again he paused and listened, and then pressed heavily until he heard a slight click. He glanced up, as directly in front of him the eye of one of the carved wooden lion's heads on the front of the board winked and slowly raised, revealing a small aperture. With a look of satisfaction, the Marquis thrust his fingers into the tiny opening and drew forth a bit of tightly folded yellow paper; he glanced at it for an instant and thrust it quickly into the pocket of his waistcoat. Then he lowered the lid of the lion's eye. There was a slight click again; and he turned, just as Dan reappeared in the doorway.

"Excuse my leaving you so abruptly," said Frost, "but I saw Jesse going off with the sleigh, and as I had given him no orders, I wanted to know where he was going. But it was all right. Are you ready, sir ? I am afraid if we stay much longer you will catch cold." This last remark was added as the Marquis politely smothered a sneeze with his flimsy lace handkerchief.

"*C'est bien,* monsieur. I fear I have taken a little cold. Perhaps it would be just as well if we explore no further to-day."

"If you prefer, sir," answered Dan, holding the door open for his guest to go out. Monsieur de Boisdhyver turned and surveyed the Oak Parlour once more before he left it. "Ah !" he exclaimed, "this so charming room—it is of a perfection ! Dorsetshire, you say ?...... To me it would seem French." They walked back rapidly along the dark cold corridors to the bar. All the way the

Marquis, wrapped tightly in his great cloak, kept the thumb of his left hand in his waistcoat pocket, pressing securely against the paper he had taken from the old cabinet in the Oak Parlour.

CHAPTER III

The household of the Inn at the Red Oak soon became accustomed to the presence of their new member; indeed, he seemed to them during those bleak winter months a most welcome addition. Except for an occasional traveller who spent a night or a Sunday at the Inn, he was the only guest. He was gregarious and talkative, and would frequently keep them for an hour or so at table as he talked to them of his life in France, and of his adventures in the exciting times through which his country had passed during the last fifty years. He was the cadet, he told them, of a noble family of the Vendée, the head of which, though long faithful to the exiled Bourbons, had gone over to Napoleon upon the establishment of the Empire. But as for himself—Marie-Anne-Timélon-Armand de Boisdhyver—he still clung to the Imperial cause, and though now for many years his age and infirmities had forced him to withdraw from any part in intrigues aiming at the restoration of the Empire, his sympathies were still keen.

When he talked in this strain, of his thrilling memories of the Terror and of the extraordinary days when Bonaparte was Emperor, Dan and Tom would listen to him by the hour. But Mrs. Frost preferred to hear the Marquis's reminiscences of the *ancien régime* and of the old court life at Versailles. He had been a page, he said, to the unfortunate Marie Antoinette; he would cross himself piously at the mention of the magic name, and digress rapturously upon her beauty and grace, and bemoan, with tears, her unhappy fate. She liked also to hear of the court of Napoleon and of the life of the *faubourgs* in the Paris of the day. On these occasions the young men were apt to slip away and leave the Marquis alone with Mrs. Frost and Nancy.

For Nancy Monsieur de Boisdhyver seemed to have a fascination. She would listen absorbed to his voluable tales, her bright eyes fixed on his fantastic countenance, her head usually resting upon her hand, and her body bent forward in an attitude of eager attention. She rarely spoke even to ask a question; indeed, her only words would be an occasional exclamation of interest, or the briefest reply.

During the day their noble guest would potter about the house or, when the weather was fine, stroll down to the shore, where he would walk up and down the strip of sandy beach in the lee of the wind hour after hour. Now and then he wandered out upon the dunes that stretched along the Neck; and once, Dan afterwards learned, he paid a call upon old Mrs. Meath who lived by herself in the lonely farmhouse on Strathsey Neck, that was known as the House of the Dunes.

After supper they were wont to gather in Mrs. Frost's parlour or in the old bar before the great hearth on which a splendid fire always blazed; and when the Marquis had had his special cup of black coffee, he would get out his violin and play to them the long evening through. He played well, with the skill of a master of the art, and with feeling. He seemed at such times to forget himself and his surroundings; his bright eyes would grow soft, a dreamy look would steal into them, and a happy little smile play about the corners of his thin pale lips. Obligingly he gave Dan lessons, and often the young man would accompany him, in the songs his mother had known and loved in her youth, when old Peter had come wooing with fiddle in hand.

But best of all were the evenings when the Marquis chose to improvise. Plaintive, tender melodies for the most part; prolonged trembling, faintly-expiring airs; and sometimes harsh, strident notes that evoked weird echoes from the bare wainscoted walls. Mrs. Frost would sit, tears of sadness and of pleasure in her eyes, the kindly homely features of her face moving with interest and delight. Nancy was usually by the table, her sharp little chin propped up on the palms of her hands, never taking her fascinated gaze from the musician. Sometimes Tom would look at her and wonder of what she could be thinking. For certainly her spirit seemed to be far away wandering in a world of dreams and of strange inexpressible emotions. For Tom the music stirred delicate thoughts bright dreams of beauty and of love; the vivid intangible dreams of awakening youth. He had not had much experience with emotion; the story of his love affairs contained no more dramatic moments than the stealing of occasional kisses from the glowing cheeks of Maria Stonywell, the beauty of the Tinterton road, as he had walked back to the old farm with her on moonlight evenings.

They would all be sorry when Monsieur pleaded weariness and bade them good-night. Sometimes his music so moved the old Frenchman that the tears would gather in his faded blue eyes and steal down his powdered cheeks; and then, like as not, he was apt to break off suddenly, drop violin and bow upon his knees, and exclaim, *"Ah! la musique! mon Dieu, mon Dieu! elle me rappelle ma jeunesse. Et maintenant — et maintenant!"* And then, brushing away the tears he would rise, make them a courtly bow, and hurry out of the room.

Dan alone did not fall under his spell. He and Tom would often talk of their strange guest after they were gone to bed in the great chamber over the dining-room.

"I don't know what it is," Dan said one night, "but I am sorry he ever came to the Inn; I wish he would go away."

"How absurd, old boy!" protested Tom. "He has saved our lives this frightful winter. I never knew your mother to be so cheerful and contented; Nancy seems to adore him, and yourself are making the most of his fiddle lessons."

"I know," Dan replied, "all that is true, but it is only half the truth. Mother's cheerfulness is costing me a pretty penny, for I can't keep her

from ordering the most expensive things,—wines,
and the like,—that we can't afford. Maybe Nance
adores him, as you say,—she is such a strange wild
child; but I have never known her to be so unlike
herself. We used to have good times together—
Nance and I. But this winter I see nothing of her
at all." For the moment Dan forgot his com-
plaint in the tender thought of his foster-sister.
"It probably is absurd," he added presently, "but
I don't like it; I don't like him, Tom! He plays
the fiddle well, I admit but he is so queer and
shifty, nosing about, looking this way and that,
never meeting your eyes. It's just as though he
were waiting, biding his time, for—I don't know
what."

"Nonsense, Dan; you're not an old woman."

"It may be, Tom, but I feel so anyway. The
place hasn't seemed the same to me since that
Frenchman came. I wish he would go away; and
apparently he means to stay on forever."

"I think you would miss him, if he were to go,"
insisted Pembroke, "for my part I'm glad he is
here. To tell the truth,Dan, he's been the life of
the house."

"He has fascinated you as he has fascinated
Mother and Nance," Dan replied. "But it stands

to reason, boy, that he can't be quite all right. What does he want poking about in a deserted old hole like Deal?"

"What he has said a thousand times; just what he so beautifully gets—quiet and seclusion."

"Perhaps you are right and I am wrong; but all the same I shall be glad to see the last of him."

The night was one of bright moonlight at the end of February. The bedroom windows were open to the cold clear air. Tom was not sleepy, and he lay for a long time recalling the dreams and emotions that had so stirred him earlier in the evening, as he had listened to the Marquis's playing. He kept whistling softly to himself such bars of the music as he could remember. Dan's chamber faced west, and Tom's bed was so placed that he could look out, without raising his head from the pillow, over the court in the rear of the Inn and into the misty depths of Lovel's Woods beyond the offices and stables.

As he lay half-consciously musing—it must have been near midnight—his attention was suddenly riveted upon the court below. It seemed to him that he heard footsteps. He was instantly wide awake, and jumped from the bed to the window, whence he peered from behind the curtain into the courtyard. Close to the wall of the Inn, directly beneath the window, a shadow flitted on the moonlight-flooded pavement, and he could hear the crumbling of the snow. Cautiously he thrust his head out of the window. Moving rapidly along near to the house, was a little figure wrapped in a dark cloak, which looked to Tom for all the world like the Marquis de Boisdhyver.

For the moment he had the impulse to call to him by name, but the conversation he had so recently had with Dan flashed into his mind, and he decided to keep still and watch. The figure moved rapidly along the west wall of the Inn almost the entire length of the building, until it arrived at the entrance of the bowling-alley which abutted from the old northern wing. Reaching this it paused for a moment, glancing about; then inserted a key, fumbled for a moment with the latch, opened the door, and disappeared within.

Tom was perplexed. He could not be sure that it was the Marquis; but whether it were or not, he knew that there was no reason for any one entering the old portion of the Inn at midnight. His first thought was to go down alone and investigate; his second was to waken Dan.

He lowered the window gently, drew the curtains across it, and bending over his friend, shook him gently by the shoulder. "Dan, Dan, I say; wake up !"

"What's the matter ?" exclaimed Dan with a start of alarm, as he sat up in bed.

"Nothing, nothing; don't make a noise. I happened to be awake, and hearing footsteps under the window, I got up and looked out. I saw some one moving along close to the wall until he got to the bowling alley. He opened the door and disappeared."

"The door's locked," exclaimed Dan. "Who was it ?"

"He had a key, whoever he was then. To tell the truth, Dan, it looked like the Marquis; though I couldn't swear to him. I certainly saw some one."

"You have not been asleep and dreaming, have you ?" asked his friend, rubbing his eyes.

"I should say not. I'm going down to investigate; thought you'd like to come along."

"So I shall," said Dan, jumping out of bed and beginning to dress. "If you really have seen any one, I'll wager you are right in thinking it's the old marquis. That is just the sort of thing I have

imagined him being up to. What he wants though
in the old part of the house is more than I can
think. He has pestered me to get back there
ever since I showed him over the place the day
he arrived. Are you ready ? Bring a candle,
and some matches. I'll just take my gun along
on general principles. I don't care how soon we
get rid of the Marquis de Boisdhyver, but I
shouldn't exactly like to shoot him out with a load
of buckshot in his hide."

Tom stood waiting with his boots in hand.
Dan went to his bureau and took out his father's
old pistol, that had done duty in the West India
trade years ago, when pirates were not romantic
memories but genuine menaces.

"Sh !" whispered Dan as he opened the door.
"Let's blow out the candle. It's moonlight, and
we will be safer without it. Be careful as you go
down stairs not to wake Mother and Nancy."

Tom blew out the candle and slipped the end
into his pocket, as he tiptoed after Dan down the
stairs. At every step the old boards seemed to
creak as though in pain. As they paused breathless half-way down on the landing, they heard no
sound save the loud ticking of the clock in the hall
below and the gentle whispering of the breeze

without. The moon gave light enough had they needed it, but each of them could have found his way through every nook and corner of the Inn in darkness as well as in broad day-light. They crept down the short flight from the landing, paused and listened at the doors of Mrs. Frost's and Nancy's chambers, and then slipped noiselessly into the bar where the logs still glowed on the hearth.

"Shall we," asked Tom in a low tone, "go down the corridor or around outside ?"

"Best outside," Dan whispered. "If we go down the corridor we are like to frighten him if he is the Marquis, or get a bullet in our gizzards if he is not. Should he be inside, he'll have a light and we can find just where he is. I have a notion that it's the Marquis and that he'll be in the Oak Parlour. We'd better creep alonge the porch."

Very softly he unlocked the door, and stepped outside. Tom was close behind him. They crept steathily along next the wall well within the shadow of the roof, pausing at every window to peer through the cracks of the shutters. But all were dark. As they turned the corner of the porch at the end of the main portion of the inn from which the north wing extended, Dan suddenly put his hand back and stopped Tom. "Wait," he breathed, "there's a light in the Oak Parlour. Stay here, while I peek in."

With gun in hand he crept up to the nearest window of the Oak Parlour. The heavy shutters were closed, but between the crack made by the warping of the wood, he could distinguish a streak of golden light. He waited a moment; and, then at the risk of alarming the intruder within, carefully tried the shutter. To his great satisfaction it yielded and swung slowly, almost noiselessly, back upon its hinges; the inside curtains were drawn; but a slight gap had been left. Peering in through this, Dan found he could get a view of a small section of the interior,—the end of the great Dorsetshire cabinet on the farther side of the room and a part of the wall. Before the cabinet, bending over its shelf, stood the familiar form of the Marquis de Boisdhyver, apparently absorbed in a minute examination of the carving. But Dan's attention was quickly diverted from the figure of the old Frenchman, for by his side, also engaged in a similar examination of the cabinet, stood Nancy. For a moment he watched them with intent interest, but as he could not discover what so absorbed them he slipped back to Tom, who was waiting at the turn of the porch.

"It's the Marquis," he whispered in his friend's ear.

"What is he up to?"

"I don't know. Apparently he is examining the old cabinet. But, Tom, Nancy is with him and as absorbed in the thing as he is. Look !" he exclaimed suddenly." They've blown out the light."

As he spoke, he pointed to the window, now dark. "Come," he said, making an instant decision, "let's hide ourselves in the hall and see if they come back."

"But Nancy—?"

"No time for talk now. Come along."

They ran back along the porch, slipped into the bar, and thence into the hall. Dan motioned to Tom to conceal himself in a closet beneath the stairway, and he himself slipped behind the clock. Hardly were they safely hidden thus, than they heard a fumble at the latch of the door into the bar. Then the door was pushed open, and the Marquis stepped cautiously in the hall. He paused for a moment, listening intently. Then he held open the door a little wider; and another figure, quite enveloped by a long

black coat, entered after him. They silently
crossed the hall to the door of Nancy's chamber.
This the Marquis opened; then bowed low, as his
companion passed within. They were so close
to him that Dan could have reached out his hand
and touched them. As Nancy entered her room,
Dan distinctly heard Monsieur de Boisdhyver
whisper, "More success next time, mademoiselle!"

There was no reply.

The Marquis turned, stole softly up the stairs,
and in a moment Dan heard the click of the latch
as he closed his door. He slipped out from his
hiding place, and whispered to Tom.

In a few moments they were back again in their
bedroom.

"Heavens! man, what do you make of it ?"
asked Tom.

"Make of it !" exclaimed Dan, "I don't know
what to make of it. It's incomprehensible. What
the devil is that old rascal after, and how has he
bewitched Nance ?"

"Perhaps," suggested Tom, more for Nancy's
sake than because he believed what he was saying, "it is simply that he is curious, and knowing
that you don't want him in the old part of the

Inn, he has persuaded Nancy to take him there at night."

"Nonsense ! that couldn't possibly account for such secrecy and caution. No, Tom, he has some deviltry on foot, and we must find out what it is."

"That should be simple enough. Ask Nance."

"Ah !" exclaimed his friend, "you don't know Nance as well as I. You may be sure he has sworn her to secrecy, and Nance would never betray a promise whether she had been wise in making it or not."

"Then go to the old man himself and demand an explanation."

"He'd lie,...."

"Turn him out."

"I could do that, of course. But I think I would rather find out what he is up to. It has something to do with the old cabinet in the Oak Parlour. I'll find out the mystery of that if I have to hack the thing into a thousand pieces. What I hate, is Nance's being mixed up in it."

"We can watch again."

"Yes; we'll do that. In the meanwhile, I am going to investigate that old ark myself. There's something about, something concealed in it, that he wants to get. When I took him in there the

day after he came, he couldn't keep his eyes off
it.   If you can get Nance out of the way to-
morrow afternoon, I'll send the Marquis off with
Jesse for that long-talked-of visit to Mondy Port;
and I'll give Jesse instructions not to get him back
before dark.   And while they are away, I'll investigate the Oak Parlour myself.   Can you get
Nance off?"

"I might ask her to go and look over the Red
Farm with me.   She might like the walk through
the woods.   I could easily manage to be away for
three or four hours."

"Good !   You may think it odd, Tom, that I
should seem to distrust Nance.   I don't distrust
her, but there has always been a mystery about
her.   Mother knows a good deal more than she
has even been willing to tell to me, or even to
Nance, I guess.   I know nothing except that she
is of French extraction, and I have sometimes
wondered since she has been so often with the
old Marquis this winter, if he didn't know something about her.   It flashed over me to-night as
I saw them in that deserted room.   Whatever is
a-foot, I am going to get at the bottom of it.   We
will watch again to-morrow night.   I heard him
whisper as he left Nance, 'More success next

time !' This sort of thing may have been going on for a month."

They undressed again, and Dan put his gun away in his bureau. "We may have use for that yet, Tommy," he said. "It would do me good, after what I have seen to-night, to put a bit of lead into the Marquis de Boisdhyver as a memento of his so delightful sojourn at *L'Auberge au Chene Rouge.*"

CHAPTER IV.

THE OAK PARLOUR

The two young men felt self-conscious and ill-at-ease the next morning at the breakfast table, but apparently their embarrassment was neither shared nor observed. Mrs. Frost had kept her room, but Nancy and the Marquis were in their accustomed places; the old gentleman, chattering away in a fashion that demanded few answers and no attention; Nancy, speaking only to ask necessary questions as to their wants at table and meeting the occasional glances of Dan and Tom without suspicion. Tom could scarcely realize in that bright morning light, that only seven or eight hours earlier he and his friend had spied upon their companions prowling about in the abandoned wing of the inn.

Monsieur de Boisdhyver assented readily enough when Dan proposed that Jesse should take him that day to Monday Port. He was curious to see the old town, he said, having heard much of it from his friend; much also from his celebrated compatriot, the Marquis de Lafayette.

Tom took occasion during the discussion to ask Nancy if she would walk across the woods with him after dinner, that he might pay a visit to the Red Farm and see that all was going well in the absence of his parents. He felt that the tones of his voice were charged with unwonted significance; but Nancy accepted the invitation with a simple expression of pleasure. When Mrs. Frost was informed of the plans for the day, she came near thwarting Dan's carefully laid schemes. She had counted upon Jesse to do her bidding and had, she declared, arranged that Nancy should help her put together the silken patches of the quilt upon which she was perennially engaged. Her foster-daughter's glance of displeasure at this was tinder to the old lady's temper, and Dan entered most opportunely.

"So !" she was exclaiming, "I am always the one to be sacrificed when it is a question of some one's else pleasure."

"Mother, Mother," Dan protested good-naturedly, as he bent over to kiss her good-morning, "aren't you ever willing to spend a day alone with me ?"

"Danny dear," cried the old lady, as she began

to smile again, "you know I'm always willing. Of course, if Tom wants Nancy to go, the quilt can wait; it has waited long enough, in all conscience. There, my dear," she added, turning to the girl, "order an early dinner, and since you are going to the Red Farm, you might as well come back by the dunes and enquire for old Mrs. Meath. We have neglected that poor woman shamefully this winter."

"Yes, Mother,—if we have time."

"Take the time, my dear," added Mrs. Frost sharply.

"Yes, Mother."

The Marquis started off with Jesse at eleven o'clock, as eager for the excursion as a boy; and by half-past twelve Nancy and Tom had set out across the woods for the Red Farm. Dan was impatient for them to be gone. As soon as he saw them disappear in the woods back of the Inn, he made excuses to his mother, and hurried to the north wing. He found the door of the bowling alley securely locked, which convinced him that either the Marquis or Nancy had taken the key from the closet of his chamber. Having satisfied himself, he went directly to the Oak Parlour.

It was cold and dark there. He opened the

shutters and drew back the curtains, letting in the cheerful midday sun, which revealed all the antique, sombre beauty of the room, of the soft landscapes and the exquisite carving of the Dorsetshire cabinet. But Dan was in no mood to appreciate the old-world beauty of the Oak Parlour. In that cabinet he felt sure there was something concealed which would reveal the mystery of the Marquis's stay at the inn and possibly the nature of his influence over Nancy. Whatever had been the object of the Marquis's search, it had not been found: his parting words to Nancy the night before showed that.

Dan took a long look at the cabinet first, estimating the possibility of its containing secret drawers. Hidden compartments in old cabinets, secret chambers in old houses, subterranean passageways leading to dungeons in romantic castles, had been the material of many a tale that Dan and Tom had told each other as boys. For years their dearest possession had been a forbidden copy of *"The Mysteries of Udolpho"* which they read in the mow of the barn lying in the dusty hay. However unusual, the situation was real; and he felt himself confronted by as hard a problem as he had ever tried to solve in fiction. He knew something about carpentry, so that his first step, after examining the drawers and cupboards and finding them empty, was to take careful measurements of the entire cabinet, particularly of the thicknesses of its sides, back, and partitions. It proved a piece of furniture of absolutely simple and straightforward construction. After long examination and careful soundings he came to the conclusion that a secret drawer was an impossibility.

Suddenly an idea occurred to him and he returned to the sitting-room. "Mother," he said, "I have been looking over the old cabinet in the Oak Parlour, thinking perhaps that I would have it brought into the dining-room. I wonder, if by chance, there are any secret drawers in it.

"Secret drawers? What an idea!" exclaimed Mrs. Frost.

"You never knew of any did you?"

"No.... Stop, let me think. Upon my word, I think there was something of the sort, but it has been so long ago I have almost forgotten."

"Try to remember, do!" urged Dan, striving to repress his excitement.

"It was not a secret drawer, but there were little hidden cubbyholes—three or four of them. I remember, now, your father once showed me how they opened. They were little places where the Roman Catholics used to hide the pages of their mass-books and such like in the days of persecution in England."

"Yes, yes," said Dan, "that makes it awfully interesting. "Did father ever find anything in them?"

"No, I think not; but, dear me, it was over thirty years ago we brought that old cabinet from England,—long before you were born, Dan."

"Can you remember how to open the secret places? I have been looking it over, but I can't see where they can be, much less how to get into them."

"There were four of them, I think; all in the carving on the front, in the eyes of the lions it seems to me, and in the lion's mouth, or in the leaves somewhere. One spring that opened them I recollect, was under the ledge of the shelf, another at the back of the cabinet and,—but no, I really can't remember where the others were."

Dan was impatient to try his luck at finding them, and hurried back to the Oak Parlour. He ran his fingers many times under the ledge of the shelf before he heard the click of a tiny spring, and, looking up, saw the lion's eyelid wink and slowly open. With an exclamation of satisfaction, he thrust his fingers into the tiny aperture, felt carefully about, and was chagrinned to find it empty. "More success next time, *monsieur le marquis!*" he muttered.

At length he found the spring that released the eyelid on the carved lion on the other side of the panel. He glanced into the little opening and, to his delight, saw the end of a bit of paper tucked away there. He dug it out with the blade of his pocket knife and unfolded it. It was yellow and brittle with age, covered with writing in a fine clear hand. But he was annoyed to discover, as he bent closely over to read it, that it was written in French, still worse, part of the paper was missing, for one side of it was ragged as if it had been torn in two.

Remembering with relief, that Pembroke had acquired a smattering of French at Dr. Watson's school for the sons of gentlemen, he put the paper carefully away in his pocket to wait for Tom's assistance in deciphering it. Then he set to work to find the missing half.

He fumbled about at the back of the cabinet for a spring that would release another secret cubbyhole, and was rewarded at last by an unexpected click, and the seemingly solid jaws of the lion fell apart about half-an-inch. But the little aperture which they revealed was empty. Further experiment at last discovered the fourth hiding place, but this also contained nothing.

It occurred to him then that the Marquis had already discovered the other half of the paper, and like himself was searching for a missing portion. As he stood thinking over the problem, he suddenly noticed that the room was in deep shadow, and realized that the sun had set over the ridge of Lovel's Woods. The Marquis would soon be returning. Carefully closing the four openings in the carving he pushed the old cabinet back against the wall, closed the shutters and drew the curtains. Then with a last glance to see that all was as he found it, he went out and closed the door the precious bit of paper in his inside pocket.

He went directly to Mrs. Frost's parlour. "Mother," he said, "please don't tell anyone that I have been in the north wing today. I have good reasons which I will explain to you before long. Now, I shall be deeply offended if you give the slightest hint."

"Gracious! Dan, what is all this mystery about?"

"You will never know, mother, unless you trust me absolutely. Mind! not a word to Tom, Nancy or the Marquis."

"Very well, Danny. You know I am as safe with a secret as though it had been breathed into the grave."

Dan did not quite share his mother's confidence in her own discretion, but he knew he could count on her devotion to him to keep her silent even where curiosity and the love of talk would render her indiscreet. He also knew, and had often deplored it, that fond as she was of Nancy she was not inclined to take the girl into her confidence.

Having said all he dared to his mother, Dan went to his room and carefully locked up the mysterious paper. He returned to the first floor just as the Marquis and Jesse drove up in the sleigh to the door of the inn.

Monsieur de Boisdhyver was enthusiastic about all that he had seen—the headquarters of General Washington, the house in which the Marquis de Lafayette had slept, the old mill in the parade, the fort at the Narrows, the shipping, the quaint old streets.... "But, O Monsieur Frost," he exclaimed, "the weariness that is now so delightful! How soundly shall I sleep to-night!"

Dan smiled grimly as he assured his guest of his sympathy for a good night and a sound sleep; thinking to himself, however, that if the Marquis walked, he would not walk unattended. He had no intention of trusting too implicitly to that loudly proclaimed fatigue.

CHAPTER V

While Dan Frost was hunting for the secret places of the old cabinet, Tom and Nancy were picking their way across the snowcovered paths of Lovel's Woods to the Red Farm. These woods were a striking feature in the landscape of the open coast country around Deal. Rising somewhat precipitously almost out of the sea, three ridges extended far back into the country, with deep ravines between. They were thickly wooded, for the most part with juniper and pine. In some places the descent to the ravines was sheer and massed with rocks heaped there by a primeval glacier; in other parts they dipped more gently to the little valleys, which were threaded with many a path worn smooth by the dwellers on the eastern shore. Nearly two miles might be saved in a walk from the Inn to Squire Pembroke's Farm by going across the Woods rather than by the encircling road.

As they were used to the frozen country Tom

and Nancy preferred the shorter if more difficult route. They had often found their way together through the tangled thickets of the Woods or along the shores of the Strathsey River, in season accompanied by dog and gun hunting fox and rabbit or partridge and wild duck. In Tom's company Nancy seemed to forget her shyness and would talk freely enough of her interests and her doings. He had always been fond of her, though until lately she had seemed to him hardly more than a child. This winter, as so frequently he had watched her sitting in the firelight listening to the old Marquis's playing and dreaming perhaps as he also dreamed, he realized that she was growing up. A new beauty had come into her face and slender form, her great dark eyes seemed to hold deeper interests, she was no longer in the world of childhood. The mystery enveloping her origin, which for some reason Mrs. Frost had never chosen to dispel, gave a certain piquancy to the interest and affection Tom felt for her. In the imaginative tales he had been fond of weaving for his own amusement, Nancy would frequently figure, revealed at last as the child of noble parents, as a princess doomed by some strange fate to exile. He thought of these things as from time to time he glanced back at her, holding aside some branch that crossed the path or giving her his hand to help her over a boulder in the way. The red scarf about her neck, red cap on her dark hair, flashing in and out of the tangled pathway against the background of the snow-clad woods, gave a bright note of colour to the scene.

They were obliged for the most part to walk in single file until the last ridge descended over a mass of rocks to the marshes along Beaver Pond. Then having given her his hand to help her down, he kept hold of it as they went along the free path to the open meadows. The feeling of Nancy's cool little hand in his gave Tom an odd and conscious sense of pleasure.

"You have been uncommonly silent, Nance, even for you," he said at last.

"Oh, I'm always silent, Tom," she replied. "It is because I am stupid and have nothing to say."

"Nonsense, my dear, you always have a lot to say to me. But you are forever reading, thinking,.... what's it all about?"

; "Oh, I think, Tom, because I have little else to do; but my thoughts aren't often worth the telling. In truth there is no one, not even you, who particularly cares to hear them. Tom," she said,

"I am restless and discontented. Sometimes I wish I were far away from the Inn at the Red Oak and Deal, from all that I know,—even from you and Dan."

Pembroke suddenly realized that he could not laugh at these fancies, as he had so often done, and dismiss as if they were the vagaries of a child.

"Why are you restless and discontented, Nancy?" he asked seriously.

"Aren't you ever?" she questioned for reply. "Don't you ever get weary with the emptiness of it all, the everlasting round, the dullness? Don't you ever want to get away from Deal, and know people and see things and be somebody?"

"I do that, Nance. I mean to go as soon as I am a lawyer. I won't poke about Deal long after that, nor Monday Port either. I mean to set up in Coventry."

"Coventry!" exclaimed the girl with an accent of disdain. "That is just a provincial town like the Port, only a little more important because it is the capital of the state."

"Being the capital means a lot," protested Tom in defense of his ambitions of which for the first time he felt ashamed. "Men are sent to Congress from there. Nance, girl, ours is a wonderful country; we are making a great nation."

"Some people may be. None of us are, Tom. I wonder at you more than I do at Dan, for you have had more advantages. As for me, I am only a girl; there's nothing for girls but to sit and sew, and prepare meals for men to eat, and wait until some one comes and chooses to marry them. Then they go off and do the same thing some place else."

"But what have you to complain of, Nancy? you have the kindest brother, a good mother, a comfortable home....."

"The kindest brother, yes. But you know Mrs. Frost is not my mother. She doesn't care for me and I can't care for her as if she were. I have never loved any one but Dan."

"You can't help loving Dan," said Tom, thinking of his good friend. "But then, little girl, you love me too." And he pressed the hand in his warmly.

Nancy quickly withdrew her hand. "I am not a little girl. I have been grown up in lots of ways ever so long."

"But you love me?"

"I like you. Oh, Tom, the life we all lead is so futile. If I weren't a girl, I should go away."

They had reached the stile by now that led into the meadow which sloped down from the clump of poplars a hundred rods or so above, in the midst of which the Red Farmhouse stood. Instead of helping his companion over the steps in the wall, Tom stopped and stood with his back to them. "Let's stay here a minute, Nance, and have it out."

"Have what out?" she asked a trifle sharply.

"You haven't any queer wild plan in your head to go away, have you?"

"I don't know—sometimes I think I have. I dare say there are things somewhere a girl could find to do."

"But Mrs. Frost—?"

"Oh, Mother would not miss me long—she'd have Dan."

"But Dan would miss you."

"Yes, Dan might. I couldn't go, if Dan really needed me here. I think sometimes he doesn't. But, Tom, if you were in my position, if you didn't know who your parents were, if all your life you had been living on the charity of others—good and kind as they are, wonderful even as Dan has always been—you couldn't be happy. I'm not happy."

"But, Nance, what has come over you?"

"No—nothing in particular; I have often felt this way."

"But, dear, I couldn't let you go. I'd mind a lot, Nance."

She looked at him with a sudden smile of incredulity. "You, Tommy?"

"You can't go—you musn't go " Tom repeated, as he drew nearer to her.

Suddenly he reached out and seized her hands. "Don't you realize it?—I love you, Nance; I've always loved you!" He drew her close to him. She did not resist nor did she yield, but still with her eyes she questioned him. "Kiss me, Nancy," he whispered. She let him press his lips to hers but without responding to the pressure, as though she still were wondering of the meaning of this sudden unforeseen passion. But at last, caught up in its intensity, she gave him back his kisses. He took her face then between his hands and looked into it with a gaze that in itself was a caress. "Oh my sweetheart!" he said softly.

Slowly she disengaged herself. "Tom, Tom," she said, "this is foolishness. We musn't do this."

"Why not?" demanded Pembroke. "I tell you
I love you!"

"No—not that way, not that way. I didn't
mean that. Why, you foolish boy, haven't we
kissed each other hundreds of times before?"

"No, Nancy, not like that—not like this," he
added, as again he put his arm around her and
drew her face to his. And again she yielded. "Say
it—say it, Nance—you love me."

She drew back from him. "I think I must, Tom.
I don't think I could let you kiss me that way if I
didn't. But now come... Tom... dear Tom... do
come... don't kiss me again."

"But say it," he insisted, "say you love me."

"Please help me over the stile."

He gave her his hand and she sprang lightly to
the top of the steps. In a second he was by her
side, both of them balancing somewhat uncertainly on the top of the stone wall. "I won't let you
down till you say it."

"Please—".

"No—you love me?"

"Yes—there—I love you—now—".

"No, kiss me again."

"Tom—no." But the negative was weak and
Pembroke took it so.

"Now," he said, as they began to cross the meadow, "we must tell Mrs. Frost and Dan."

"Tell them what?"

"Why, that we are in love with each other, and that you are going to marry me. What else?"

"No, no," exclaimed Nancy, "You must say nothing. I am not in love. I don't mean to marry you."

"But why not? You are. You do."

"Are—do—?"

"In love—you do mean to marry me."

"No—Tom, listen—you know your father and mother would hate it. You have at least two years before you can practice. We couldn't marry —we can't marry. Oh, there are things I must do, before I can think of that."

"Not marry me? Good Lord, what does it mean when people are in love with each other, what does it mean when a girl kisses a fellow like that?"

"I don't know what it means—madness, I guess. Do you think I could marry as I am, not knowing who I am?"

"Oh, what do I care who your parents were! We'll find out. I swear we will. Good Lord, I love you, Nancy; I love you!"

"Please, please don't make me talk about it now."

"But soon—?"

"Yes, soon—only promise you'll say nothing to Dan or to Mother till we have talked again. I must think; it is all so queer and unexpected; I never dreamed that you cared for me except as a little girl."

"I didn't know I did. But come to think of it, Nance, it has been you as much as Dan that has brought me to the Inn at the Red Oak. Why it was you I wanted to walk and talk and play with."

"Please,—dear Tom—G—ive me time to think what it all means. Now be careful, there's the farmer. You have a lot to do, and we have been lingering too long. Mother wants us to go back by the dunes and enquire for old Mrs. Meath; so we must hurry."

The sun had set before they started on the homeward journey in one of the squire's sleighs. As they turned the bend at the beach and started across the dune road close to the sea, a great yellow moon rose over Strathsey Neck.

Tom had been so preoccupied with his own emotions and the unexpected and absorbing relation in which he found himself with Nancy, that he had altogether forgotten why he had asked her to go off with him that afternoon. As they skimmed along over the snow-packed road across the sands, Tom spied another sleigh on the Port road, the occupants of which he recognized as Jesse and the Marquis. Suddenly the memory of the night before flashed over him. He pointed with his whip in their direction. "There's the old Marquis coming back from Monday Port," he said.

Nancy looked without comment, but Tom thought the colour deepened in her cheeks.

"See here, Nance," he exclaimed impulsively; "has the Marquis anything to do with the mood you were in this afternoon? Has he said anything to make you discontented?"

He was sure that now she paled.

"What makes you ask?"

"Oh—a number of things. I've seen you with him more or less; felt he had some influence over you."—Tom was blundering now and knew it.—

She looked at him coldly. "I have been with the Marquis very little save when others have been about. He has no influence over me. I don't care to discuss such queer ideas."

"Oh, all right... I dare say I'm mistaken... I

only thought..." He hesitated... "If you care for
me, I don't mind what you think of the Marquis."

"Remember, Tom—you promised to say nothing until I gave you leave. You're not fair..."

"But you do love me?"

Nancy was silent.

"There is nothing between you and the old
Frenchman—no mystery?"

There was no reply. Nancy sat with compressed
lips and drawn brows, gazing fixedly at the distant
House on the Dunes at the end of their road. For
a long whilte they drove on in silence.

At the House on the Dunes they chatted for a
while with old Mrs. Meath, who lived there alone
with a maid-of-all-work. She was a source of
much anxiety to Mrs. Frost, who sent several
times each week to learn if all was going well. But
Mrs. Meath was a Quaker and apparently never
gave a thought to loneliness or fear.

"They will never guess," she said to Nancy and
Tom as they sat in the tiled kitchen talking with
her, "what I am going to do."

"Not going to leave the House on the Dunes,
Mrs. Meath?"

"Deary me! no; but I am going to take a
boarder."

"Really?—you are setting up to rival the Inn, eh?" said Tom.

"No, Tommy, nothing of the sort. But I am offered good pay for my front room, and as Jane Frost is always nagging me about living here alone, I thought I'd take her."

"And who pray is your new boarder?" asked Nancy.

"That is the funny part of it," replied Mrs. Meath, "I know nothing but her name — Mrs. Fountain. Everything has been arranged by a lawyer man from Coventry, and she is coming in a few days. Tell thy mother, Nancy dear, that she need worry about me no longer."

"I will, Mrs. Meath. I think it is a splendid idea, and I hope you will like the lady. Mother will be so glad that you have some one with you."

Soon they were on their way across the dunes and marshes to Tinterton road and home. ~~Dan~~ Tom was preoccupied, not with the news that was so exciting to Mrs. Meath, but with the recollection of his conversation with Nancy as they had driven toward the house. Despite her implicit denial he knew there was a secret between the Marquis de Boisdhyver and herself. He could not imagine what it might be, and it was evident that she did not mean to tell him at present. But his anxieties on this or kindred subjects were not relieved by his companion during the remainder of the drive. Moreover his attempts to speak again of his newly discovered passion were received coldly—so coldly indeed that he had no heart for pleading for such proofs as she had given him earlier in the afternoon that she shared his emotion. So despite the splendid moon, the bright cold night, the merry jangle of the sleigh bells, the drive back was not the unmixed joy Tom had promised himself; and he felt his role of a declared and practically-accepted lover anything but a satisfactory one.

Finally they reached the Inn and entered the bar where they found the Marquis sitting alone before a cheerful fire. All of Tom's suspicious jealousies returned with fresh force, for Nancy rapidly crossed the room, spoke a few words to the old gentleman in an inaudible tone of voice, and passed quickly on to her own apartments.

PART II

THE TORN SCRAP OF PAPER

CHAPTER VI

THE HALF OF AN OLD PAPER

That evening Mrs. Frost made a particular request for music. Poor Dan, impatient to be alone with Tom and show him the torn scrap of paper that he had found that afternoon was forced to bring out his fiddle and accompany the Marquis. Tom, for first part, was more concerned with his own relations with Nancy than with the mysterious possibilities of the previous night. The poignant notes of the violin set his pulses to beating in tune with the throbbing of the music and transported him again into the realms of youthful dreams. They were quaint plaintive songs of old France that the Marquis chose to play that evening, folk tunes of the Vendée, love songs of olden time.

From where he sat in the shadow Tom got a full view of Nancy seated on the oaken setlle near the fire. Her brows were drawn a little in deep thought, her lips for the most part compressed, though ever and anon relaxing at some gentler thought. Her hands were clasped, her head was bent a little, but her body was held straight and tense. Her eyes, dark and lustrous in the light of the flaming logs, always fixed upon the musician, not once wandering in his direction.

What was the influence, the fascination that strange old Frenchman seemed to exert? It seemed to Tom impossible that there could be a secret which she felt necessary to hide from them, her lifelong friends. But apart from what he knew had taken place the night before as he looked back over the past month, he was conscious that there had been a change in Nancy, a change that mystified him. It was the danger in this change, he told himself, that had awakened in him the knowledge of his love.

But then as he looked across at her so lovely, in the firelight, he felt again the thrill as when first he had taken her hand that afternoon. In that moment all the dreams, the vague longings of his boyhood had found their reality.

Suddenly, while he was thinking thus, the Marquis laid his violin upon his knees. "Ah, *ma jeunnesse!"* he exclaimed in a dramatic whisper, *"et maintenant—et maintenant!"*

For a moment no one spoke or stirred. They looked at him curiously as they always did when he brought his playing to an end in such fashion. Then he rose. *"Bon soir, madame; bon soir, messieurs; bon soir, mademoiselle."*

Tom saw his little faded blue eyes meet Nancy's with a look of swift significance. Then he bowed with a flourish that included them all.

"A thousand thanks, Monsieur le Marquis," murmured Mrs. Frost, "how much pleasure you give us!"

They all rose then, as the Marquis smiled his appreciation and withdrew.

"Give me your arm, Dan," the old lady said. "It must be past my bedtime. Come, Nancy."

"Yes, mother." The girl rose wearily, stopping a moment at the mantelpiece to snuff the candles there. Tom seized his opportunity, and was by her side. She started, as she realized him near her.

"Nance, Nance, I must have a word with you," he exclaimed in a tense whisper, "don't go!"

"Nance, come," called Mrs. Frost from the hallway.

"Yes, Mother, I am coming... I must go, Tom. Don't delay me. You know how Mother is..."

"What difference will it make if you wait a moment? Good Lord! Nance, I have been trying all evening to get a word with you, and you have not so much as given me a glance. Don't go— please don't go! Oh, Nancy dear,—I love you so!"

He seized her hands and kissed them passionately. "Nance, Nance... please..." His arms were about her.

"Tom, you make it so hard... Remember, you promised me... No word of love until I can think, until I have time to know... Please, Tom, let me go."

"I can't let you go. Oh sweetheart dear."

"Tom, we musn't—Dan, Mother...!

Unheeding her protest, he put his arms around her. An instant he felt her yield, then quickly thrusting him aside, she ran from the room, leaving him standing alone there, trembling with excitement, chagrin, happiness, alarm.

In a moment his friend returned and Tom pulled himself together. "Come on," said Dan, "I have a lot to tell you."

"Did you find anything this afternoon?" exclaimed Pembroke.

"Sh! for heaven's sake be careful. Don't talk here. Let's go upstairs."

A few minutes later they were closeted in Dan's chamber. The curtains were tightly drawn and a heavy quilt was hung over the door. Good Lord! thought Tom, could it be possible that these precautions in part at least were taken against Nancy. The world seemed to have turned upside down for him in the last twenty-four hours.

"Aren't we going to keep watch to-night?" he asked.

"Yes, but later. They are just getting to bed —or pretending to. Look here, this may throw light on the mystery. I found this paper in a secret cubby-hole in the old cabinet in the Oak Parlour. Draw a chair up to the table so that you can see."

"The cabinet," he continued, as he took the paper out of his strong-box and began to unfold it, "was brought from some old manor house in England. It has four little secret cubby-holes, opened by hidden springs, that Mother says were probably used by the Roman Catholics to hide pages of their mass-books during the days of persecu-

tion.   She remembered fortunately a little about
them. They were all empty but one, and in that
I found this torn scrap of paper."

He handed the yellowed bit of writing to Tom,
who flattened it out on the table before him.

"Why it's written in French," Pembroke exclaimed, as he bent over to examine it.

"Yes, I know it is," said Dan. "I can't make
head or tail of it. Besides it seems to be only a
part of a note or letter. I could hardly wait to
give you a chance at it. You can make something
of it, can't you?"

"I don't know—I guess I can. It's hard to read
the handwriting. The thing's torn in two—
haven't you the rest of it?"

"No, I tell you; that's all I could find; that's
all, I am sure, that can be in the cabinet now. My
theory is that the old marquis has somehow come
across the other half and is still looking for this.
God only knows who hid it there.

"How the deuce could the Marquis know about
it. Ah! look—it's signed somebody, something
de Boisdyver—'ancois—that's short for Francois,
I guess. Evidently 't wasn't the Marquis himself.
Wonder what it means?"

For goodness' sake, try to read it."

"Wait. Get that old French dictionary out of the bookcase downstairs, will you? I'll see if I can translate."

Dan crept softly out, leaving Tom bent over the paper. Again he smoothed it out carefully on the table, bringing the two candles nearer, and tried to puzzle out the faint fine handwriting.

"I can make out some of it," he remarked to Dan, when his friend returned with the dictionary. "Let me have that thing; there are a few words I don't know at all, but I'll write out as good a translation as I can."

While Tom was busy with the dictionary, Dan placed writing materials to his hand, and sat down to wait as patiently as he could. His curiosity was intensified by Pembroke's occasional exclamations and the absorption with which he bent over the task.

"There!" Tom exclaimed after half-an-hour's labour, "that's the best I can do with it. You see the original note was evidently torn into two or three strips and we have only got the righthand one, so we don't get a single complete sentence—, but what we have is mighty suggestive. Listen— This is what it says: Make great efforts.. gap.. glorious, I am about to leave'...gap... 'to offer my'

...gap...'that I should not return'...gap...'directions'
...gap...'this paper which I tear'..gap...'the explanation'...something missing...'to discover'... that's the
end of a sentence   The next one begins, 'This
treasure'.. than another gap.. "jewels and money'..
"secret chamber'...'one can enter'... something gone
here...'by the *salon de chene*'—that's the Oak
Parlour, I suppose...something missing again...'by
a spring'...'hand of the lady in the picture'... 'chimney on the north side of the'...'side a panel which
reveals'...'one will find the directions'...more missing...'of the treasure in a golden chest'...That's the
end of it. And, as I said before it is signed,--ancois
de Boisdhyver."   There, you can read it.   That's
the best I can make of it."

Dan bent over his friend's translation. "Whoever wrote it was about to leave here to offer
something to somebody, and if he did not return,
apparently he is giving directions, in this paper,
which he tears in to two or three parts, how to discover—a treasure?—jewels and money, I guess,—
that he is about to hide or has hidden in a secret
chamber, which is entered in some way from the
Oak Parlour—?..pushes a spring,—Something to
do with the hand of the lady in the picture, near
the chimney on the north side of the room...then

a panel which reveals...where?... the directions will be found, for getting the treasure, in a golden chest in the secret chamber? How's that for a version? I reckon the other half doesn't tell as much...'ancois de Boisdhyver!.—That can't be the Marquis, for none of his names end 'ancois; do they? Let's see, what are they? — Marie, Anne, Timélon, Armand...Tom,"—and Dan faced his friend excitedly,—"that old devil is after treasure! Who the deuce is 'ancois de Boisdhyver, and how did he come to leave money in the Oak Parlour? Hanged if I believe there's any secret chamber! By gad, man, if I didn't hurt when I pinch myself, I'd think I was asleep and dreaming. What do you make of it?"

"Pretty much what you do. Somebody sometime,—a good many years ago, concealed some valuables here in the Inn. It must be some one who is connected with our marquis, for the last names are the same. These are directions, or half the directions, for finding it. The Marquis knows enough about it to have been hunting for this paper. Who the devil is the Marquis?"

"The Lord knows. But how does Nance come in?"

"Blamed if I can see; wish I could! This ac-

counts for the Marquis's mysterious investigations, anyway. Probably he's no right to the paper. Maybe he isn't a Boisdhyver at all. I'll be
damned if I can understand how he has got Nance
to league with him."

"And now what the deuce are we going to do
about it?" asked Dan.

"Hunt for the treasure ourselves, eh?"

"Well, why not? but to do that we've got to get
rid of the Marquis. He'll be suspicious if we begin
to poke about the north wing. Hanged if I would-
n't like to have it all out with him!"

"Yes, but we'd better think and talk it over
before we decide to do anything. We can watch
them. We'll watch to-night any way, and plan
something definite to-morrow."

"I tell you one thing, Tom, I am going to make
Mother tell me all she knows about Nancy. Perhaps she is mixed up in some way with all this.
But it's time to keep watch now. We'll put out
the candles and I'll watch for the first two hours.
If you go to sleep, I'll wake you up to take the
next turn. How about it ?"

"Hang sleep!" Tom replied.

"All right, but we must blow out the light.
Lucky it's clear. Let's whisper after this."

Tom threw himself on the bed, while Dan sat near the window and kept his eyes fixed on the door of the bowling-alley. They talked for some time in low tones, but eventually Tom fell asleep. Dan waked him at twelve for his vigil, and he in turn was wakened at two. During the third watch they both succumbed to weariness.

Tow awoke with a start about four, and sprang to the window. The moon was sinking low in the western sky, but its light still flooded the deserted courtyard beneath. He heard the patter of a horse's hoofs on the road beyond and the crunching of the snow beneath the runners of a sleigh. Well, he thought, as he rubbed his eyes, it was too near morning for anything to happen, so he turned in and was soon asleep, as though no difficult problems were puzzling his mind and heart and no mysteries were being enacted around him.

CHAPTER VII.

A DISAPPEARANCE.

When Dan came downstairs in the morning Mrs. Frost called him to the door of her bedroom. "What on earth is the matter with Nancy?" she exclaimed; "I have been waiting for her the past hour. No one has been near me since Deborah came in to lay the fire. Call the girl Danny; I want to get up'.'

"All right, mother. She has probably overslept; she had a long walk yesterday."

"But that is no excuse for sleeping till this time of day. Tell her to hurry."

"It is only seven, mother."

"Yes, Danny, dear, but I mean to breakfast with you all this morning if I ever succeed in getting dressed."

Dan crossed the hall and knocked at Nancy's door. There was no response. He knocked again, then opened the door and looked within. Nancy was not there, and her bed had not been slept in.

He went back to his mother. "Nancy is not in

her room," he said. "She has probably gone out for a walk. I'll go and look for her."

He went to the kitchens to enquire of the maids, but they had not seen their young mistress since the night before.

"Spec she's taken dem dogs a walkin'," said black Deborah unconcernedly. "Miss Nance she like de early morn' 'fore de sun come up."

Dan went out to the stables. The setters came rushing out, bounding and barking joyously about him.

"Have you seen Miss Nancy this morning, Jess?" he asked.

"No, Mister Dan, ain't seen her this mornin'. Be n't she in the house?"

"She doesn't seem to be. Take a look down the road, and call after her, will you? Down, Boy; down, Girl!" he cried to the dogs.

Dan began to be thoroughly alarmed. If Nancy had gone out, the dogs would certainly have followed her. She must be within!

He went back into the house, and searched room after room, but no trace of her was to be found. He returned at last to his mother's chamber.

"I can't find Nancy," he said. "She must have gone off somewhere."

"Gone off! why, she must have left very early then. I have been awake these two hours—since daylight—; I would have heard every sound."

"Well, she isn't about now, Mother. She will be back by breakfast time, I don't doubt. Just stay abed this morning, I will send her to you as soon as she comes."

"I shall have to, I suppose. Really, Dan, it is extraordinary how neglectful of me that child can sometimes be. She knew—"

"Mother, don't find fault with her. She is devoted to you, and you know it."

"I daresay she is. Of course she is, and I am devoted to her. Where would she be, I wonder, if it hadn't been for me? Good heavens! Dan, can anything have happened to her?"

"No, no—of course not,—nothing."

"Search the house, boy; she may be lying some place in a faint. She isn't strong—I have always been worried—"

Don't get excited, Mother. We will wait until breakfast time. If she doesn't turn up then, you may be sure I shall find her."

He looked at his watch. It was already nearly

eight o'clock, so he decided to say nothing to Pembroke until after breakfast. He found the Marquis and Tom chatting before the fire in the bar.

"Shall we have breakfast?" said Dan. "Mother will not be in this morning."

"Ah!" exclaimed the Marquis, as they took their seats at table, "that is a disappointment. And shall we not wait for Mademoiselle Nancy?"

"My sister has stepped out, monsieur; she may be late. Shall I give you some coffee?"

"If you please—. We have another of these so beautiful days, eh? This so glorious weather, these moonlight nights, this snow— *C'est merveilleux.* Last night I sat myself for a long time in my window. Ah *la nuit* — the moon past its full, say you not?—the sea superbly dark, superbly blue, the wonderful white country! As I sat there, messeurs, a sight too beautiful greeted my eyes. A ship, with three great sails, appeared out on the sea and sailed as a bird up the river to our little cove. *Voila, mes amis,"*—he waved his hand toward the eastern windows—"She is anchored at our feet."

The two young men looked in the direction in which the marquis pointed, and to their astonishment they saw, riding securely at her moorings in the cove, a large sailing vessel. She was a three-masted schooner of perhaps fifteen hundred tons, a larger ship than they had seen at anchor in the Strathsey for many a year.

"By all that's good!" exclaimed Tom, "that is exactly the sort of ship my father used to have in the West Indie trade, a dozen or fifteen years ago. What is she? I wonder; and why is she anchored here instead of in the Port?"

The Marquis shrugged his shoulders. "That I can tell you not, my friend; but I am happy that she is anchored there for the hours of beauty she has already given to me. On this strange coast of yours one so rarely sees a sail."

"No, they go too far to the south... But what is she?" asked Dan. "We must find out." He went to the cupboard, and got out his marine glass and took a long look at the stranger.

"What do you make her out?" asked Tom.

"There are men on deck, some swabbing out the roundhouse. One of them is lolling at the wheel. She flies the British flag."

"Do you, perhaps, make out the name?" asked the Marquis.

"I don't know—yes," Dan replied, twisting the lens to suit his eyes better and spelling out the letters, "S,O,U,T,H,E,R,N,C,R— the *Southern Cross*. By Jingo, Tom, we'll have to go down to the beach and have a look at her."

Tom took the glasses; turning them over presently to the Marquis. "She is a good fine boat, eh?" exclaimed M. de Boisdhyver, as he applied his eye to the end of the glass.

"She certainly is," said Dan.

They sat down at length and resumed their breakfast. The ship had diverted Tom's attention for the moment from the fact that Nancy had not appeared.

"Where is Nance, Dan?" he asked at length, striving to conceal his impatience.

"I don't know," Dan replied. "I think she has gone over to see Mrs. Meath and stayed for breakfast."

"Madame Meath—?" enquired the Marquis.

"At the House on the Dunes," Dan answered, a trifle sharply.

"A long walk for Mademoiselle on a cold morning," commented Monsieur Boisdhyver, as he sipped his coffee.

In a few moments Dan rose. "Going to the Port to-day, Tom?"

"Not till later, any way; I am going down to the beach to have a look at that ship."

"Wait a little, and I'll go with you." He turned to the door and motioned Tom to follow him.

Outside he took his friend's arm and drew him close. "Tom, something's up; Nancy's not here."

"Nancy's not here;" exclaimed Pembroke. "What do you mean? Where is she?"

"To tell the truth, I don't know where she is; her bed has not been slept in. I thought at first she had gone for a walk with the dogs as she does sometimes, but Boy and Girl are both in the barn. It's half-past eight now, and she ought to be back."

"Good Lord! man, have you searched the house?"

"I've been over it from garret to cellar."

"And you can't find her?"

"Not a sign of her."

"Have you been through the north wing?"

"Yes, all over it. I have been in every room in the house, boy. Nance isn't there. You heard nothing in the night, did you?"

"Nothing."

"When did you go to sleep?"

"Perhaps about half-past three. Come to think

of it, I awoke at four with a start, for I heard
a sleigh on the Port Road. After that I went to
bed."

"The sleigh hadn't been at the Inn?"

"It couldn't have been—I'd have heard of it
if it had; you see it woke me up just going along
the road."

"I don't suppose we need worry. But it is
queer—none of the servants have seen her since
last night."

"My God, what can have happened to her?"
cried Tom.

"Sh, boy! We have nothing to go on, but I
wager that old French devil knows more than he
will tell."

"Then, we'll choke it out of him."

"No, no, don't be a fool! She may be back any
minute. I'll get the sleigh and go over to the
House on the Dunes. In the meanwhile don't
show that you are anxious! I'll be back inside of
an hour, and we can have a look at the ship. If
Nance isn't with Mrs. Meath, why I am sure I'll
find her here. Let's not worry till we have to."

Tom assented to this proposition somewhat un-
willingly. Despite his friend's reasuring words,
he did not feel that Nancy would be found at the

House on the Dunes or that she would immediately return. He remembered her telling him of her
desire to go away. He remembered how strangely
she had received the declaration of his love, and
he feared almost as much that she had fled from
him, as that the Marquis, weird and evil as he began to think him, had any hand in her disappearance.

After Dan's departure in the sleigh, Tom wandered about restlessly. When half an hour passed
and Frost did not return, he went out to look down
the road and see if he were coming. The white
open country was still and empty, and the only
sign of life was the great three-masted ship riding
at anchor in the cove, with seamen lolling about
her deck.

As Tom stood under the Red Oak, the Marquis
stepped out of the front door. He was wrapped
in his great coat, about to take his morning walk
up and down the gallery.

"Why so pensive, Monsieur Pembroke? Is it
that you are moved by the beauty of the scene—,
the land so white, the sea so blue, and the *Southern Cross* shining as it were in a northern sky!"

Tom grunted a scarcely civil reply, and turning

away to avoid further conversation, strolled down the avenue of maples toward the road.

Monsieur de Boisdhyver raised his eyebrows slightly, and began his walk. By and by, still more impatient, Pembroke walked back toward the house. If Dan did not return soon, he determined he would go after him. As he came up to the gallery again the Marquis paused and spoke to him. "And Mademoiselle, she has not returned?" he asked.

"No!" Pembroke replied sharply. "She has gone to the House on the Dunes and her brother has driven over to fetch her."

"Ah! pardon," exclaimed Monsieur de Boisdhyver; "I did not know... But it is cold for me, Monsieur Pembroke; I seek the fire."

Tom did not reply. The Marquis went inside, and presently Tom could see him standing at the window, the marine glass in his hands, sweeping the countryside.

Pembroke passed an anxious morning. Ten o'clock came; half-past; eleven struck. Nancy had not appeared, or was there a sign of Dan. Unable to be patient longer, he set out on the Port Road to meet his friend.

CHAPTER VIII

GREEN LIGHTS

The smoke was curling from the chimneys of the House on the Dunes as Dan drove up the long marsh road from the beach. He had half convinced himself that Nancy would be there, and he hoped that she herself would answer his knock. When at length the door was opened it was not by Nancy nor by Mrs. Meath, but by a stranger whom he had never seen before.

"Yes?" a pleasant voice questioned, but giving an accent to the monosyllable that made Dan think instantly of France.

He found himself facing a charming woman, her bright blue eyes looking into his with a smile that instantly attracted him. She was well-dressed, with a different air from the women he knew. And she was undeniably pretty—of that Dan was convinced, and the conviction overwhelmed him with shyness. He stood awkward and ill-at-ease; for the moment forgetting his errand. "I suppose," he stammered, "—I beg your pardon—but I sup-

98

pose you are Mrs. Meath's new boarder, — Mrs. Fountain?"

"Yes," replied the strange lady with an amused smile, "that is what I imagine that I am called. My name is Madame de La Fontaine. And you—?"

"I? — Oh, yes—of course—I am Dan Frost from the Inn over yonder. I came to see Mrs. Meath to ask if my sister Nancy is here."

"Alas!" replied Madame de La Fontaine, "poor Mrs. Meath she this morning is quite unwell. She is in her room, so that I am afraid you cannot see her. But, I may tell you, there is no one else here, just myself and my servants."

"You have not seen or heard anything then of my sister, Nancy Frost?" repeated Dan.

"Nancy Frost?—your sister?—No, monsieur. I am arrived only last night and have seen no one."

"I had hoped my sister would be here. I am sorry about Mrs. Meath; perhaps I can be of some service. If you should need me at any time, I can almost always be found at the Inn at the Red Oak."

"The Inn at the Red Oak?" repeated Madame de La Fontaine, "and is that near by?"

"It is about a mile and a half by the road,"

Frost replied, "but you can see it plainly from the doorstep here."

The foreign lady stepped out in the crisp February air. "Can you point it out to me? I may need your assistance some time."

"You see the woods and the oak at the edge of them," said Dan, pointing across the Dunes. "That great tree is the Red Oak, the rambling old building beneath it is the Inn."

"Ah! one can see quite plainly from one house to the other, is it not so?"

"Quite," Dan replied.

"Thank you, monsieur. I trust there will be no need for assistance. But it makes one glad to know where are neighbours, especially—" she added, "while poor Mrs. Meath is ill."

As she spoke she turned to the door with the air of dismissing him, but on second thoughts she faced him again. "I wonder, Mr. Frost, will you do me a favour?"

"I shall be delighted," Dan exclaimed.

"My luggage arrived last night," said Madame de La Fontaine, "upon the ship that is at anchor in the bay. They are to bring my boxes ashore. But before that I desire to give directions to the captain at the beach, and I cannot well do so by my servant. Will you be kind enough to walk with me and show me the way?"

Dan forgot about Nancy in his eagerness to assure this unusually attractive lady that he was at her disposal. She disappeared within, and he heard her give some quick, sharp directions in French to a maid. Then in a moment she reappeared on the little porch, bonneted and wrapped for a walk in the cold.

As they set out across the Dunes, she kept up a rapid fire of questions that might have seemed inquisitive to one more accustomed to the world than Dan. He found himself in the course of that quarter of an hour talking quite freely with the charming stranger.

"No, I did not make the journey from France in the *Southern Cross*," she replied to one of his interrogations, "that would have been uncomfortable, I fear. But she brings over my boxes. She is arrived somewhat sooner than I was promised."

"Do you expect to signal her from the beach?"

"But yes."

"How will they know who you are?"

"Oh, they have instructions. You must think all this curious!" she commented with a smile. "You must think me an odd person."

The possible oddness of Madame de La Fontaine made less impression upon Dan than did her charm. He was conversing easily with a very lovely woman, and all else was forgotten in that agreeable sensation.

As they emerged from the Dunes upon the little beach of the Cove, Dan observed on the deck of the *Southern Cross* a sailor watching them through a glass. Madame de La Fontaine drew her handkerchief from beneath her cloak and waved it toward the ship.

"This is the signal," she explained, "that they were instructed to look out for. If I am not mistaken Captain Bonhomme will come to the shore for my directions. You speak French, monsieur?"

"Not at all," Dan replied.

"Ah!" sighed the lady, "you lose a great deal."

"I might have learned some this winter," said Dan; "for we have had a French gentleman as our guest at the Inn."

"Indeed! And who, may I ask, is your French gentleman?"

"His name is the Marquis de Boisdhyver. Do you, by any chance, know him?"

"The Marquis de Boisdhyver?" repeated Madame de La Fontaine. "I know the name certain-

ly; it is an old family with us, monsieur. But I
do not recall that I have ever had the pleasure of
meeting any one who bore it... But see! they are
lowering the boat."

They were now at the edge of the surf. Madame de La Fontaine again waved a hand in the
direction of the clipper. Dan saw a small boat
alongside her, into which several sailors and an
officer, as it seemed, were clambering over the rail.
They pushed off, and began to row vigorously for
the shore.

The French lady stood watching them intently.
Within a few moments the little boat was beached,
the officer sprang out, advanced to Madame de La
Fontaine, and saluted. She exchanged sentences
with him in French of which Dan understood
nothing. Then the seaman touched his cap, got
into his small boat, and gave orders to push off.

"He understands no English," remarked Madame de La Fontaine. "I gave directions about
my boxes. We may return now, monsieur; or
doubtless I am able to find my way back alone."

"Oh no," exclaimed Dan gallantly, "I will go
with you."

The lady smiled graciously. As they walked
back across the Dunes, she kept up a lively con-

versation, no longer asking him questions, nor, he observed, giving him the opportunity to ask any.

At the door of the House on the Dunes she dismissed him finally. "I am but too grateful, Monsieur, for your kindness. I hope that we shall meet again while I dwell in your beautiful country. In the meantime, I trust you will find your sister."

Dan flushed, how could he have forgotten Nancy! Taking the hand that his new acquaintance offered, he hurried away. He met Tom on the Port Road about half a mile from the Inn and was truly worried to find that Nancy had not returned; he explained briefly his own delay in his expedition with the strange lady to the beach.

"It is certainly odd, though perhaps not so odd as stupid, that they should have anchored in the Cove just to disembark one woman's boxes. It would have been much simpler to go to the Port, as every well-bred skipper does, and had the French woman's stuff carted out. At any rate, we'll go down this afternoon and have a look at her."

By the time they reached the Inn it was noon, and still there was no word of Nancy. The dinner was a silent one, as the Marquis tactfully did not disturb his companions' preoccupation, and Mrs. Frost, who was unusually nervous, did not appear.

After the meal the two young men started for the beach. At Tom's suggestion they got a little dory from the boathouse and rowed out to the clipper. The wind had shifted to the southeast, but still there was not enough of a sea to give them any trouble; and in a few minutes they were under the bows of *The Southern Cross*. Dan hailed a seaman who was leaning over the gunwhale and watching them with idle curiosity. If the man replied in French, it was in a variety of that tongue that Tom's limited attainments did not understand, and, annoyed by the incomprehensible replies, he asked for "le captaine". At length,—possibly attracted by the altercation at the bows,—the authoritative-looking person who had come ashore in the morning in response to Madame de La Fontaine's signal, now appeared at the gunwale and glanced below at the two young men in the dory. His expression betrayed no sign that he recognized Frost. Indeed he vouchsafed no syllable of reply to the questions Dan asked in English or to those that Tom ventured to phrase in Dr. Watson's French.

He was not, they thought, an attractive person; his countenance was swarthy, his eyes were black his hair was black, his heavy jaw was shadowed by an enormous black mustachio. A kerchief of brilliant red tied about his throat gave him the appearance of the matador in a Spanish bullfight rather than the officer of an English merchantman. He glanced at the dory occasionally, shook his head silently in response to the requests to go aboard, and at length when that did not serve to put an end to them, he shrugged his shoulders and disappeared. The seaman continued to lean over the gunwale and spat nonchalantly as though that were the measure of their appreciation of this unasked-for visit.

"I move we skip up the rope," said Tom, "and explain ourselves at close quarters."

"Thanks, no," replied Dan. "Either of those two amiable gentlemen looks capable and willing of pitching us overboard. The water is too cold for bathing."

"Very well," said Tom, "I will yield to your sober judgment for the moment; but I propose to see the inside of that ship sooner or later unless she weighs anchor in the hour and sails away. But we ought to be getting to town to make enquiries about Nancy. For Heavens' sake, Dan, where do you suppose she can be?"

They rowed back to the beach, stowed the dory in the boathouse, and set out in the sleigh for Monday Port. Diligent enquiry there, in likely and unlikely places, proved fruitless. It was night-fall when they returned to the Inn.

They were greeted by the Marquis in the bar. "Mademoiselle Nancy, she has not been found?"

"No," said Dan. "I take it from your question that she has not come home yet either."

"She is not come, no. Perhaps she stays at the House on the Dunes?"

"I do not know," Dan answered tartly. I expect her every moment, but it is idle to conceal from you, Monsieur, that we are much concerned as to her absence."

The Marquis grew sympathetic,—optimistically sympathetic. Tom clutched at his re-assuring words, but Dan was even more irritated by the silence that Monsieur de Boisdhyver had maintained throughout the day.

Directly after supper Dan went into his mother's parlour, leaving the others to their own devices. The Marquis settled himself near the fire and was soon absorbed in reading an old folio; Tom wandered restlessly about, now up and down the long bar, now in the corridors, now on the gallery and in the court without.

The night, after the bright day, had set in raw and cold; a damp breeze blew from the southwest, and gave promise both of wind and rain. From his position under the Red Oak, Tom could see the red and green lights of *The Southern Cross* at her moorings in the Cove below, and across the Neck the lighted windows of the House on the Dunes. Over all else the night had cast its black damp mantle.

As he stood watching, deeply anxious for the welfare of the girl he loved, he noticed a new light appear in one of the upper windows of the House on the Dunes—not yellow as is the light of candles, but green like the light on the port side of the clipper in the Cove. Had he not seen the lights from the other windows he could have thought it was another ship on the ocean side of the Neck.

He looked for a long time at the tiny spark in the distance, wondering what whim had induced Mrs. Meath to shade her candles with so deep a green. As he strolled back toward the Inn, he glanced through the windows of the bar where the Marquis still read by the fireside. Suddenly the old gentleman, as Tom curiously watched him, laid his book down on the table and rose from his chair. He looked about the room and then advanced to the window. Tom instinctively slipped behind the trunk of the great oak. Monsieur de Boisdhyver stood for several moments peering into the darkness. Then he turned away and crossed the room to the door into the front hall. It flashed through Tom's mind that possibly the Marquis had started on another of his mysterious tours. He ran down again into the court far enough from the house to command a view of the entire facade, and watched curiously, particularly the north wing. All was dark, save for the lights below.

Suddenly he saw the flicker of a candle in one of the windows, not of the north wing, but of the south. A moment's glance, and he made sure that it was the room occupied as a sleeping apartment by Monsieur de Boisdhyver.

The Marquis was standing by the window, with his face pressed close to the pane, peering out into the night. He still held the candle in his hand. To Dan's surprise, he placed it carefully on the broad window-sill, and drew down the dark shade to within a foot of the sill, blotting out all save a narrow band of light. Then the Marquis disappeared for several moments into the interior of the room. Dan was about to turn back into the house, when again Monsieur de Boisdhyver came to the window. He did not raise the shade, but inserted between the windowpane and the candle a strip of dark green paper. It was translucent and had the effect of sending a beam of green light southward, across the meadows and the dunes, to meet—Tom suddenly realized—the rays of the green light from the House on the Dunes.

Was it a signal being exchanged, and between whom? The coincidence of green lights from the Inn and the House on the Dunes, at the same moment, was too marked to be without significance. To what end was the Marquis de Boisdhyver exchanging myterious signals with some one in that lonely farmhouse, and what did they mean?

Tom repressed his agitation and remained for some time watching the two green lights that glowed toward one another over the dark landscape.

Suddenly the light in the House on the Dunes was extinguished; then, momentarily it shone again, but quickly went out and left the great sweep of dunes in darkness. Two minutes later the same thing took place in the window of the south chamber of the Inn. The light flashed and was gone, flashed again and shone no more.

Tom went in, by a rear entrance, to the bar. The Marquis was seated by a table, absorbed in reading. He started as Tom entered. "Still no word of Mademoiselle?" he piped.

"Still no word, monsieur," Pembroke answered laconically. He also seated himself in the candle light and took up the last issue of the *Port News*.

"Do you know what has become of Dan?" Pembroke asked presently.

"Monsieur Frost he has been closeted with madame his mother for the past half-hour. You have no further plans for seeking Mademoiselle? For myself, I grow alarmed."

"I know nothing but what you know, monsieur. Nancy has not returned. There has been no word of her. We shall have to wait." With tremendous effort to conceal his agitation and annoyance, Tom resumed his reading.

Monsieur de Boisdhyver glanced at him for a moment with a little air of interrogation, then shrugged his shoulders slightly and turned again to his French paper.

CHAPTER IX

After the long day of fruitless search and enquiry for the vanished Nancy, supper being over and Tom having gone outside, Dan joined his mother in the blue parlour.

Mrs. Frost was weary with waiting and anxiety, but as Dan threw himself on a couch near her chair, she watched him patiently.

"There is no clue, Dan?" she ventured at last.

"No clue, mother, not the slightest. Nancy seems to have vanished as completely as if she had dissolved into air. As you know, the house has been thoroughly searched; the servants carefully questioned; and enquiries have been made at every conceivable place in Monday Port. I have been to the House on the Dunes, and to the farmhouses on every road round about. No one has seen or heard of her. She has taken French leave, but for what reason I can't imagine."

"Nancy has not been happy for some time, Dan," said Mrs. Frost.

"No, I have fancied that she was not. But why? Do you suppose she has left us deliberately? or—". He paused uncertain whether or not to give voice to his suspicions.

"Or what?" asked his mother.

"Or she has been forced away against her will."

"Against her will!" the old lady exclaimed. "Who could have forced her? and for what reason? Do you think she may have been kidnapped?"

"Either kidnapped or decoyed away."

"But who could have designs upon Nancy? It is more reasonable to suppose that she left of her own accord. I confess that would not altogether surprise me."

"I don't know, mother, but I have my fears and suspicions. There may be some one who has a deep interest in Nancy, who for reasons of his own, which I don't yet understand, may wish to control her movements. I wish you would tell me all you know of Nancy's origin. You have never told me;—you have never told her, I fancy,—who she really is and how you came to adopt her as your own child. I have never been curious to know, in fact I have not wanted to know, for she has always been to me precisely what a sister of my own blood would be. But now, it may help me to understand certain strange things that have happened in the last few days."

For a moment Mrs. Frost was silent. "No, I have never spoken to you or to Nancy of her early history, Dan; simply because, to all intent she has been our own. I have always wished that she should feel absolutely one with us; and I think she always has, until this winter. But of late I have noticed her discontent, her growing restlessness, and I have sometimes wondered if she could be brooding over the mystery of her early years. But she has never asked me a direct question; and I have kept silent."

"I think now, mother," Dan replied, "it is your duty to tell me all you know."

"I have no reason, my dear, to keep anything from you. I should have told you years ago, if you had asked me. There is not much to tell. You may remember when you were a boy about six or seven years old, a French exile came to the Inn, a military gentleman, who had left France in consequence of the fall of the great Napoleon."

"Yes, I remember him distinctly," said Dan. "He used to tell stories to Tom and me of his adventures in the wars. Tom was speaking of him only the other day."

"Well," continued Mrs. Frost, "this gentleman called himself General Pointelle. I learned afterwards it was not his real name. Who he actually was, I have not the slightest idea. He brought with him a little girl two years old, a sweet little black-eyed girl, to whom I, having lost your only sister at about that age, took a great fancy. The General also had two servants with him, a valet, and a maid. The maid, a pretty young thing, took care of the child. They arrived in mid-summer, on a merchantman that plied between Marseilles and Monday Port. I do not know why General Pointelle came to this part of the country, or why he chose to stay at the Inn; at any rate he came, and he engaged for an indefinite period the best suite of apartments in the old north wing. He had the Oak Parlour—"

"The Oak Parlour!" exclaimed Dan.

"Yes," replied Mrs. Frost, "that was part of the suite reserved usually for our most distinguished guests. The general used that for a sitting-room and the adjoining chamber as a bed-room. The maid and child occupied connecting rooms across the hall. The valet, I believe, was in some other part of the house. General Pointelle proved himself a fascinating guest, and his little daughter

Eloise was a favourite with all the household. The maid, pretty as she certainly was and apparently above her station, I somehow never trusted. I have always believed that the relations between the general and herself were not what they should have been. But Frenchmen look at such things differently, I am told; and it was not to our interests to be over-curious.

"They had been with us about two months when one fine morning we awoke to find that General Pointelle, his valet, and the charming Marie had disappeared, and little Eloise was crying alone in her big room. You have probably guessed the child was Nancy."

"Yes," Dan agreed, "but do you mean that the father actually abandoned her?"

"Practically. He left a note for me and a little bag of gold amounting to two thousand dollars to be used for the child. If you will hand me that old secretary there, I will show you the letter."

Dan placed the old-fashioned writing-desk on the table beside her, and waited anxiously while she fumbled in her pocket for the key. She unlocked the desk, and after searching a few moments amongst innumerable papers, drew out an old letter. This she unfolded carefully and handed to Dan. It was written in English, in a fine running hand. He read it attentively.

> "*The Inn at the Red Oak, Deal*:
> "14 October, '814.

"Madame:

"Political circumstances over which I have no "control, patriotic considerations which I cannot "withstand, demand my immediate return to "France. In the conditions into which I am about "to be plunged the care of my dear little daughter "becomes an impossibility. Inhuman as it must "seem to you, lacking in all sense of Christian du- "ty as it must appear to you, I entrust, without "the formality of consulting you, my beautiful lit- "tle Eloise to your humane and tender care. With "this letter I deposit with you the sum of two "thousand dollars in gold, which will go a little "way at least to compensate you for the burden I "thus unceremoniously, but of necessity, thrust "upon you. I appeal to and confide in the good- "ness of your heart, of which already I have such "abundant testimony, that will take pity upon the "misfortune of a helpless infant and an equally "helpless parent. May you be a mother to the

"motherless, and may the Heavenly Father bless
"you for what you shall do.

"I embark, madame, upon a dangerous and un-
"certain mission. Should that mission prove suc-
"cessful and restore the fortunes of my house, I
"will return and claim my daughter. Should fate
"overwhelm me with disaster, I must beg that you
"will continue to regard her and love her as your
"own. The issue will have been decided within
"five years. Permit me to add but one thing more,
"—in the event that I fall in the cause I have em-
"braced, I have made arrangements whereby com-
"munications shall be established with you, ma-
"dame, that will redound to your own good for-
"tune and that of the little Eloise.

"All effort to thwart my plans or to establish my
"identity in the meantime, will, I must warn you,
"be fruitless.

"Adieu, madame: accept the assurance of my
"gratitude for all that you have already done to
"sweeten exile and of my earnest prayer for the
"blessing of God upon your great good heart.

"I remain, madame, for the present, but always,
"under whatever name,

"Your grateful and sincere servant,

"GASTON POINTELLE."

As Dan, with gathering brows, concluded the reading of this extraordinary letter, Mrs. Frost resumed her story.

"We always imagined that the general and his companions had sailed in a French vessel that lay at that time in the Passage and left that morning at dawn. There was nothing to do but adopt little Eloise Pointelle for my own. I changed her name, at your father's suggestion, to Nancy Frost; knowing that Pointelle was not the general's real name. For five years we looked to see our guest return; and afterwards for years, we hoped to receive some communication that would prove, as he promised, of advantage to Nancy and ourselves. But from the night General Pointelle left our house to this day, I have not heard one word to show that he still existed or, indeed, that he ever had existed. We brought Nancy up as our own daughter, though, never concealing from her the fact that she was not of our blood. Indeed, Dan, I have loved her dearly."

"Certainly, you have always treated her with the greatest kindness. But this is quite extraordinary, Mother. I think it will throw light on Nancy's present disappearance."

"Do you think the father is alive, Dan? that he has communicated with her?"

"Not that, mother; I am really in the dark. But I believe that the Marquis de Boisdhyver has some connection with your General Pointelle, and that his stay with us this winter has something to do with Nancy."

In response to Mrs. Frost's questions, he told of the meetings of Nancy and the marquis, but decided to say nothing about the paper that he had found in the Oak Parlour.

"I want you to be careful, Mother, to give no hint to the Marquis that we suspect him in any way. Tom and I are trying to solve the mystery, and secrecy is of the greatest importance. It is a more complicated business than we imagined. I must go now and find Tom. May I keep this letter?"

"Yes, but keep it under lock and key. I have guarded it for sixteen years; and it is the only evidence I possess of Nancy's origin."

Dan returned to the bar, where he found the Marquis and Tom still reading their papers.

"Ah!" exclaimed Monsieur de Boisdhyver, "I trust, Monsieur Frost, you bring us the good news at last of the return of Mademoiselle."

"Unfortunately, I do not, monsieur," Dan replied. "Our efforts to find out what has become of her have been entirely unsuccessful. I am very anxious, as you may imagine."

"And to what mishap do you attribute Mademoiselle's so unceremonious departure?"

"I do not attribute it to any mishap," replied Dan. "I think that my sister has gone off on a visit to some friends, and that her messages to us have been miscarried. I feel certain that to-morrow we will be completely reassured."

"Ah! I hope so with all my heart," exclaimed the Marquis fervently. "It is a matter of deep distress to me—monsieur. But if—to-morrow passes and still you do not hear—?"

"God knows, sir. We must do everything to find her."

"We shall find her," cried Tom, as he sprang to his feet, unable longer to repress his anxiety or his irritation. "And if we do not find her safe and well, woe to the man who has harmed her."

"Bravo!" cried the Marquis. "Permit me to adopt those words to express my own sentiments. I applaud this determination, monsieur, *de tout mon coeur.*"

Tom glared at the little old man with an ex-

pression of illconcealed rage. He was about to
blurt out some angry reply, when a warning gesture from Dan checked him. Without speaking,
he flung himself out of the room.

"Poor Tom!" said Dan quickly, to cover Pembroke's attitude toward the Marquis, "this takes
him especially hard. He is in love with Nancy."

"*Eh bien!* I sympathize with his good taste.
It is that that accounts for his vigour of his ex-
pressions, so much more *emphatique* than our
good host."

"More emphatic, perhaps," said Dan, "though
I do not feel less strongly."

The Marquis made a little bow, as he rose to
retire. "If, chance, monsieur could require my
assistance—"

"Thank you," said Dan quickly. "In that case,
sir, I shall be only too happy to call upon you."
He rose also, and courteously held the candle till
the Marquis had reached the top of the stairs.

Tom waited his friend impatiently in their
common chamber. And when at last, having
closed the house for the night, Dan joined him,
he told at once of the signals which he supposed
had been exchanged between the Marquis at the
Inn and someone at the House on the Dunes. In

return Dan repeated what he had learned about Nancy from Mrs. Frost.

"There is no doubt in my mind," said Dan, "that the Marquis knows all about Nancy's disappearance and where she is, and further I believe that Nancy's disappearance is part of a plot with the Marquis here, Madame de la Fontaine at the House on the Dunes, and that schooner riding at anchor in the Cove. I have a plan, Tom."

"Go ahead for heaven's sake. If we don't do something, I'll go in and choke the truth out of that old reprobate. He applauds my sentiments, eh! Good God! If he knew them!"

"Yes, yes," said Dan. "But the time for choking has not come. You nearly gave yourself away to-night, you will ruin our plans, and involve Nancy in some harm. She is probably in that old villain's power. Now listen to me. The first thing to do is to discover Nancy's whereabouts. The second is to get at the bottom of the Marquis's plot and the secret of the torn scrap of paper. We will find the clew to both, I think, if we can discover the meaning of the signals between the Marquis and the lady in the House on the Dunes."

"Right!" cried Tom. "But how?"

"One of us must stay at the Inn and watch the Marquis to-night, and the other investigate the House on the Dunes. I have already been there and made the acquaintance of the lady, so I had better do that, and you stay here. Do you agree?"

"Yes, of course; though I envy you the chance to be out and doing."

"You will be doing something here. I want you to hide yourself in the hallway near the Marquis's door and watch all night—till dawn anyway. He cannot get out of his room without coming into the hall, and we must know what he does to-night. If the Marquis can spend a sleepless night, we can afford to do so. I don't know what I can do at the House on the Dunes but I shall take the pistol, and you can keep my gun. To-morrow I will get more arms, for I shouldn't be surprised if we needed them. Is everything clear?"

"Perfectly," said Tom. "I'll watch as soon as you are off."

"Good-night, old boy, good luck."

"Good-night," and Dan slipped out of the room and down the dark stairs.

CHAPTER X

As soon as Dan had gone Tom blew out his light and slipped into the hallway.

This portion of the Inn was simple in design. A long corridor ran through the middle of the house to meet a similar passage at the southern end extending at right angles to the main hall. The South Chamber, occupied by the Marquis de Boisdhyver, opened into the southwest passage, but the door was well beyond the juncture of the two corridors. It was Pembroke's intention to conceal himself in the bedroom next the Marquis's chamber, from the door of which he could look down the entire length of the main hall, and by stepping outside get a view of the branch hallway into which the door of this room and that of the Marquis actually opened. A further advantage was that the windows of this room, like those of the South Chamber, looked out upon the Dunes and the Cove.

As Tom stepped from his chamber, the house

125

seemed utterly deserted; save for the roaring of the wind without and an occasional creak or crack in the time-worn boards, there were no sounds.

The night was not a dark one, although the wind was rising and rain was threatening; for a full moon lurked behind the thick veil of cloud and something of its weird weak light relieved the darkness even of the great corridor of the Inn.

Tom stole softly down the hallway and gained the room next the Marquis's. He took his position in a great chair, which he drew near the open door, and laid his gun on the floor near at hand. No one could enter the hall without his seeing him. Every few moments he would tiptoe to the doorway, thrust his head into the corridor, and listen intently for any sound in the South Chamber.

It was a lonely and unpleasant vigil. The night was wild, the storm was rising, the old Inn was moaning as though in distress; and, despite his natural courage, fantastic terrors and dangers thrust themselves upon his excited imagination. He would much have preferred, he felt, to be out in the open as Dan was, even facing real dangers and greater difficulties. Deeper than by these imaginary fears of the night, he was racked with anxiety to know what had become of the girl he loved. Had she been decoyed away by the evil genius of the place; was she in danger? Had she disappeared of her own free will; and didn't she really love him?

He was not in the least sleepy; but after a while the vigil began to tell upon his nerves. He found it almost impossible to sit still and wait, perhaps in vain. He made innumerable trips across the room to the windows to look out into the bleak night. The landscape was blotted out. Not a light showed from the House on the Dunes; only the two lamps on the schooner at anchor in the Cove gleamed across the night. Eleven o'clock, twelve o'clock struck solemnly from the old clock on the stairs.

Once as he was looking out of the window, it seemed to him that the green light on the *Southern Cross* was moving. But it was impossible that she should weigh anchor in the teeth of the rising storm. He was mistaken. Nay, he was sure. But it was rising, slowly, steadily, as though drawn by an invisible hand, to about the height of the masthead. There at last it stopped, and swung to the wind, to and fro, to and fro; high above its red companion, high above the deck.

And then, suddenly, as if to answer this mysterious manoeuvre, the green light, that earlier in the evening had glowed from a north window of the House on the Dunes, now flashed from an east window of the old farmhouse; flashed, then gleamed steadily. The light on the *Southern Cross* was lowered slowly, then raised again. The light in the House on the Dunes vanished; soon flashed again and then vanished once more. Slowly the light in the schooner descended to its normal position. A moment later the green light appeared on the north side of the House on the Dunes, where it had been earlier, and shone there steadily.

Was it a signal to the Marquis de Boisdhyver? Tom tiptoed to the partition between his room and the South Chamber, and put his ear to the wall to listen. Not a sound reached him. He turned to the door to go into the corridor, and stood suddenly motionless. For there, advancing ever so cautiously down the hall, carrying a lighted candle in his hand, was the old Marquis. He was clad in night dress and cap, with a gayly-coloured dressing-gown worn over the white shirt. Slowly, silently, pausing every instant to listen; he stole on, gun in hand, and Tom followed him as cau-
Tom and Dan.

tiously and as quietly. Instead of turning to the right at the partition that divides the north and south wings of the Inn and going down stairs, the Marquis turned to the left, into the short hall that led directly to the great chamber occupied by

By the time Pembroke in pursuit had reached the turn and dared to peep around the corner of the wall, the Marquis was at the door of Dan's room. He stood there, ear bent close to the panel, intently listening.

Tom waited breathless. Not satisfied, Monsieur de Boisdhyver turned about and went into an adjoining chamber, the door of which stood open. Pembroke was about to advance, when the Marquis emerged again into the corridor, having left his lighted candle in the empty room. This manoeuvre, whatever advantage it had for the Marquis, was fortunate for Pembroke, for it left the end of the little hall, where he stood watching, in deep shadow. He could now step boldly from behind the concealing wall without fear of immediate detection.

Again the Marquis stood and listened at the door of Dan's room, then cautiously turned the knob. The door yielded and opened an inch or so. Monsieur de Boisdhyver put his ear to the crack.

Dissatisfied with the absolute silence that must have met him, he pushed open the door a little further and thrust his head inside. In a moment he disappeared within.

Tom realized that the Marquis would soon discover the fact that the room was empty. He looked about quickly for a place of concealment that would command a view of all the halls. Fortunately the partition that divided the long corridor between the north and south wings was hung with heavy curtains. Deciding instantly, Pembroke slipped behind them, and ruthlessly slit an opening in the thick green stuff, through which he could peed out. He was just in time, as the Marquis came out of their bedroom and softly closed the door. He stood irresolute; then, with even greater caution, re-entered the room in which he had left his candle. To Tom's chagrin, the candle was suddenly extinguished and the Inn left in darkness.

For some moments, there was absolute silence. Then Tom could hear faintly,—or feel rather than hear—the Marquis cautiously finding his way back. Luckily, the old Frenchman was groping his way next the other wall. Pembroke slipped from behind the curtains and stole softly in pursuit. As he reached the south end of the corridor, he heard the latch of the Marquis's door click softly. Alarmed by discovering that they were not in bed, thought Tom, he had abandoned whatever purpose he had in mind for his midnight prowl.

After waiting a little and hearing no more, Tom went again to the window. The rain had begun now and the wind was blowing a gale. Suddenly Pembroke discerned a light shining from the window next the very one from which he was peering into the darkness,—the steady glow of a deep red light.

"Another signal!" he murmured; then waited to see if it would be answered by the House on the Dunes. Perhaps fifteen minutes passed, and then, suddenly, there gleamed through the rain and dark, a tiny bit of red flame, just where the House on the Dunes must be. A little later the red lamp on the *Southern Cross* performed a fantastic ascension to what Pembroke took to be the masthead.

The red light in the neighbouring window was extinguished. Almost instantly the red spark on the Dunes disappeared, and in a few moments the schooner's lamp began its descent. Sumultaneously they glowed again and the ship's light danced upward; then the two red lights on shore vanished and the lamp on the *Southern Cross* sank to its proper place and stayed there.

Of one thing Tom was sure: The Marquis, the lady at the House on the Dunes, and the skipper of the schooner in the Cove, were in collusion. Of another thing he felt almost equally certain: the red light was a signal of danger, and the message of danger flashed across the night was the fact that he and Dan were not safe asleep in bed.

For a long time he watched, keen with excitement; listened patiently; started at every sound. But nothing more unusual did he hear that night than the roar of the wind, the dash of the brawling southeaster against the panes, and the groans of the old house, shaken by the storm. Toward morning he crept back to bed and fell instantly into a deep and dreamless sleep.

While Tom was thus watching and sleeping a somewhat different experience had fallen to the lot of Dan Frost. He had no definite plan in making a midnight visit to the vicinity of the House on the Dunes, but he hoped to discover some clue to the surrounding mysteries. From time to time during the day he had taken his field glasses to one of the upper rooms of the Inn, and scanned the countryside but nothing unusual seemed astir in the white world without. The *Southern Cross* had lain on the surface of the little cove all day, swaying with wind and tide, no sign of activity upon her decks. It was after ten when he started forth. The night was not quite dark, for the full moon was shining somewhere behind the thick veil of clouds. Earlier in the evening Dan had intended to go boldly to the House itself and demand an interview with old Mrs. Meath; but he reflected that he would probably be met with the excuse that Mrs. Meath was ill, and he did not know how he could force himself in, particularly past the barrier of Madame de la Fontaine's charming manner.

It was an unpleasant walk with the wind in his face, and it was nearly eleven before he turned into the long dune road, which branched from the Port Road near the Rocking Stone and led directly to the old farmhouse on Strathsey Neck. To his chagrin it appeared that all lights had been extinguished as if the inmates of the house had gone to bed.

The old farmhouse loomed before him, dark and forbidding. On either side there were outhouses, and in the rear quite near the house a barn.

There was not a tree on the place; indeed, there was little vegetation upon the entire Neck, save the grass of the middle meadows which in summer furnished scant nourishment for the cattle and a flock of sheep. Now all was bleak and covered with snow, and a freshening gale swept out of the great maw of the Atlantic.

Keeping close to the fence, Frost began to make a complete circuit of the farmhouse. As he turned a corner of the south end, or rear of the house, he was relieved to see a light burning in the kitchen. He stole cautiously to a position within the shadow of the barn from which he could get a glimpse of the interior. In the kitchen standing before a deal table, he saw a young woman—not Jane, Mrs. Meath's maid-of-all-work, but a stranger,—with her hands deep in a bowl of dough. Her back was toward him, but he guessed that she was Madame de la Fontaine's maid, whom he had seen in the morning. The door into the dining-room beyond stood open, and by craning his neck, Dan could see that the room was lighter, but he could not discover whether or not it were occupied. The shutters of the dining-room were so closely barred and the curtains so tightly drawn that not a ray of light penetrated to the outside.

The girl in the kitchen proceeded busily about her work. She was evidently engaged, despite the lateness of the hour, in mixing bread.

Once while he waited patiently, to what end he hardly knew, Madame de la Fontaine entered the kitchen. She was clad in black and held in her hands what Dan took to be a ship's lamp. She stood for a moment in the doorway and spoke to the servant maid. The girl stopped her work, and taking a strip of paper, ignited it at a candle and lighted the lamp, which Madame de la Fontaine held up for her. It glowed instantly with a deep green flame, such as Tom had described as shining from a window of the House on the Dunes in the early evening.

As soon as her lamp was lighted Madame de la Fontaine left the room. Supposing that she was about to give a signal, Dan's heart leaped at the prospect of some result to his eavesdropping, and he stole carefully around to the front of the house. Presently from an upper window in the east side of the house, not the north as he had expected, he saw the green light sending forth its message across the Dunes—to whom? Probably the signal could be seen from the Inn, but it more likely was intended for the schooner in the Cove.

Sure enough, as he watched, Dan saw the phe-
nomenon of the ascending lamp on the *Southern
Cross,* which at that identical moment Tom Pembroke was watching from his post of vantage in
one of the south windows of the Inn.

A little later the signal was removed from the
east window of the farmhouse and placed in a
north window. Dan looked to see the answering
gleam from the Inn at the Red Oak. But none
came. Crouched in a corner of the fence, he waited perhaps for half-an-hour.

Suddenly a signal gleamed from the Inn, but
this time it was not green as he expected, but red.
In a few moments a form appeared in the window
of the farmhouse, and a white hand, which he supposed was that of Madame de la Fontaine, took
hold of the lamp and reversed it, so that now it
showed red. The light in the Inn vanished, reappeared, vanished again. The same thing happened to the light in the House on the Dunes.
And looking eastward, Dan saw the ship's red
lamp perform its fantastic ascent and descent.
Soon all was left in darkness. Frost slipped back
to his post near the barn and looked again into the
kitchen.

Madame de la Fontaine was standing in the

doorway as before. The maid, turning away from the table, came at that moment to the window, and raised the sash, as though she were over-heated. Presently, leaving the window open, she turned to her mistress, and Dan could hear the sharp staccato of her voice as she said something in what seemed to him her barbarous French.

Impelled by curiosity, he crept closer to the house. He was within six feet of the window, standing on the tip of his toes. Suddenly he felt himself pinioned from behind; his arms were gripped as in a vise, a hand grasped his throat and began to choke him, and a sharp knee was planted with terrific force in the small of his back. He made a gurgling sound as he went backward, but there was no opportunity for struggling. He re-covered from the shock to find himself stretched at full length in the wet snow. Some one was sitting upon him, struggling to thrust a gag into his mouth; some one else was binding his hands and feet.

He could just distinguish, in the sickly moon-light and the dim rays of the candle from the kitchen, the faces of his assailants. One was the murderous looking Frenchman, the skipper of the *Southern Cross*, the other he took to be a common seaman.

Attracted by the scuffle, the French maid had
thrust her head out of the window and was addressing the combatants in vigorous French.
Neither then nor later did Madame de la Fontaine appear. When Frost was safely bound and
gagged, Captain Bonhomme arose, said a few
words to his companion, and disappeared into the
farmhouse. Dan's guard searched him rapidly,
confiscated his revolver and knife, and then resumed his seat upon his legs. Inside the kitchen
Dan could hear the sounds of an animated French
dialogue, in which he imagined from time to time
that he detected the silvery tones of Madame de la
Fontaine's voice. Perhaps fifteen minutes elapsed.
Captain Bonhomme came out of the house, strode
to the spot where Dan was lying, and addressed
him in excellent English.

"Monsieur; for purposes which it is superfluous
to explain, it is decided to extend to you for a
while the hospitality of my good ship the *Southern
Cross*,—a hospitality, I may say, that your unceremonious eavesdropping has thrust upon you.
I will release your feet; and then, monsieur, you
follow my good Jean across the sands. If you are
quiet, no harm shall come to you. If you resist,
cher monsieur, it will be of painful duty that I en-

trust the contents of this revolver into—*mais non! Vous comprenez, n'est-ce pas?—Bien!*"

He gave a sharp order to the seaman. The handkerchief about Dan's ankles was untied, and he was roughly assisted to his feet.

"The snow is wet, eh! Yes, for the good wind is moist. Now, *Allons!*"

Jean led the way, and Dan, deciding that he had no choice in the matter, followed obediently. The captain brought up the rear. As they went out through the gate, Dan turned for a moment and looked back at the house. He could see the French maid still at the kitchen window. At the same moment Captain Bonhomme glanced back and ceremoniously raised his hat.

"*Bonsoir, mam'zelle.*"

"*Bonsoir, monsieur,*" was the sharp reply, and the window was lowered with a bang.

They went on in silence across the Dunes to the beach. There, drawn up above high water line, they found a skiff. The captain and Jean shoved off, sprang in, and the little boat plunged into the combing waves. They reached the *Southern Cross* without misadventure. The captain blew a call upon a boatswain's whistle. A rope was lowered and Jean made the skiff fast to the ladder at the schooner's side. The captain took out his revolver and held it in his hand, while Jean unloosed the cords that bound Dan's wrists.

"Now up, *mon ami*."

For a moment Dan thought of risking a scuffle in the unsteady skiff, but discretion proved the better part of valour, and he climbed obediently on to the deck. The seaman stood close by till the captain and Jean had clambered up after him. A few words in French to his men, then Captain Bonhomme, beckoning to Dan to follow, led the way down the companion. He opened the door of a little cabin amidships and bade Frost enter.

"You will find everything required for your comfort, monsieur," he said, "and I trust you will make yourself at home, as you say; and enjoy a good night and a sound sleep. We can discuss our affairs in the morning."

And with the words, he closed the door, turned the key in the lock, and left Dan to his reflections.

PART III

THE SCHOONER IN THE COVE.

CHAPTER XI

THE SOUTHERN CROSS

Dan spent a miserable night. He had soon satisfied himself that escape was impossible. A child could not have squeezed through the port hole, and the stoutness of the door—barred, he fancied, as well as locked on the outside,—seemed to indicate that this particular cabin had been constructed for the purpose of keeping an enemy out of mischief.

Young Frost's reflections, as at length he stretched himself upon the bunk, were anything but agreeable. The reconnoitre at the House on the Dunes had established nothing but what they already practically knew—that the Marquis, the lady, and the captain of the schooner were working together. If they were responsible for Nancy's disappearance, as Dan was convinced, he had not succeeded in getting a scrap of evidence against them. And to cap the climax, he had stupidly allowed himself to be captured. The method of his capture seemed to him quite as ignominious as the fact.

He was not particularly alarmed for his own safety. He did not doubt that eventually he would escape, though at the moment he could not imagine how; or, failing in that, he supposed he would be released,—honorably discharged, as it were,—when it was too late for him to interfere with the designs of the conspirators. And this was the bitterest reflection of all: that a carefully-planned conspiracy was on foot, and no sooner had he and Tom realized it than through sheer stupidity he must not only make it clear to the Marquis and his colleagues that they were being watched, but must let himself fall into their power. Poor Tom! thought Dan ruefully as he tossed upon the little bunk, there must fall upon him now the brunt of whatever was to be done for Nancy's rescue, for the thwarting of whatever nefarious designs this gang of French desperados were concocting.

Escape! A dozen times and more he sprang

from his bed to press his face against the thick glass of the little port and to rage futilely that he could not elongate his six feet of anatomy, and slip through. In vain he would throw his weight against the door, without so much as shaking it. And then he would sink back upon the bunk and determine to conserve his strength by snatching a bit of sleep. And he would wait—since he must wait—till morning.

The gale had lashed itself into a fury; the rain was pouring in torrents; and the ship rolled distressingly in the rising sea. It was near dawn before Dan succeeded in getting to sleep at all, but from then on for several hours he slept heavily. When he awoke the storm, like many storms that come out of the south, had exhausted itself. The rain had ceased, the wind had fallen, and it was evident from the motion of the ship, that the sea was going down. Dan sprang to the port hole and peered out, and was thankful to realize that the peep hole of his prison gave upon the shore.

Though it had stopped raining, the clouds were still grey and lowering, and the morning light was weak and pale? The Dunes, beyond the disturbed waters of the little cove, looked dirty and bedraggled. The snow had been washed off the hills the little streams that here and there emptied into the Cove had swollen to the size of respectable brooks, and the high water of the night had strewn the beach with brown tangled seaweed. There was no sign of human life in evidence. Dan could just see the upper story of the House on the Dunes, but no other habitation save the deserted fisherman's huts that straggled along the beach.

His watch showed half-past seven when the evil-visaged Jean unbarred the door, opened it about a foot, and thrust in upon the floor a tray of food. Dan sprang forward and succeeded in getting his foot into the opening, so that Jean could not close the door. He was prepared to fight for his liberty. Despite Jean's superior strength, Dan had the advantage in that his own body acted as a lever, and for a moment it seemed that he was to be successful; but the Frenchman, with a violent execration, suddenly let go his hold on the knob, the door swung in, and Dan fell back on all fours upon the floor. By the time he had recovered himself for another dash, he was confronted by Jean, a disagreeable leer upon his unpleasant countenance and a cocked pistol in his hand.

Dan stood in his tracks. "I want to see Captain Bonhomme!" he demanded, making up in the tone of his voice for the vigor his movements suddenly lacked.

"Je ne parle pas englais," was the irritating reply, as Jean, menacing the prisoner with the pistol, reached for the door and closed it with a snap. Dan had the chagrin of hearing the key turn in the lock and the heavy bar fall into place across the panels.

He sat down ruefully, but after a moment or so took up the tray and placed it on the bunk before him. He made a bad breakfast off thick gruel, black bread and villainous coffee, and then kicked his heels impatiently for an hour or more.

Eventually Jean reappeared, this time pistol in hand, and behind him, to Dan's relief, Captain Bonhomme. The captain entered the little cabin, leaving the door open behind him while Jean stood in the passage on duty as guard. The swarthy unattractive face of Captain Bonhomme wore this morning an expression of sarcastic levity that was more irritating to Frost than its ferocious anger had been the night before.

"Bon jour, monsieur," said the captain in a tone of obnoxious pleasantry. "I trust the night has gone well with you."

"You will oblige me," snapped Dan for reply.

"by omitting your hypocritical courtesy. I demand to know what you mean by this proceeding, —capturing me like a common thief and imprisoning me on this confounded ship?"

Captain Bonhomme's countenance quickly lost its factitious cheerfulness. "Monsieur," he replied sharply, "I did not come to you to bandy words. If you will reflect on the occupation you were indulging last night at the moment we surprised you, you will comprehend that it was certainly to be inferred that, if you were not a thief, you were an eavesdropper; which, to my way of thinking, is as bad. If you address me again in that insulting tone, I shall leave you till such a time as you may be willing to listen at least with common courtesy to what I have to say. You are, young gentleman, a prisoner on my ship and very much in my power. You have grossly offended a distinguished countrywoman who is under my protection in your barbarous country. Madame de la Fontaine, however, has been good enough to interest herself in your behalf and to beg that I shall not unceremoniously pitch you overboard to feed the fishes as you so richly deserve."

Dan bit his lips, but for the moment kept silent.

"I am come this morning," continued Captain Bonhomme, "not for the pleasure of entering upon a discussion, but to inform you that a little later in the morning, when this infernal wind of yours has blown itself out, Madame de la Fontaine proposes to come aboard. For reasons of her own, she does you the honor to desire a conversation with you. I have to ask that you will meet my distinguished patroness as the gentleman you doubtless profess to be, and that you will give me your word not to attempt to escape while Madame is on board the ship."

"I shall not give my word," protested Dan, "under any circumstances to a pirate such as I take you to be."

"*Eh bien, monsieur;* in that case, you will appear before Madame in irons. From your window, so admirably small, you will see at what hour Madame comes aboard. If in the meantime you have decided to give us your word of honour, well and good; if you continue to display your freedom of choice by the exercise of your stupidity, also, well and good. And now, *au revoir.*" Captain Bonhomme smiled grimly, bowed again with insulting politeness, and left Dan alone in the cabin.

An hour, two hours passed. The wind had abat-

ed, the sun was struggling to dissipate the murky
bank of cloud that hung from zenith to the eastern
horizon.   From his coign of vantage at the little
port hole Dan saw Madame de la Fontaine pick
her way across the Dunes and come upon the little
beach. A small boat had put off from the schooner
and was being rowed to shore by two seamen. The
French lady gathered her skirts about her ankles,
and stepped lightly into the skiff, as the men held
it at the edge of the surf. The little boat was then
pushed off and rowed briskly toward the *Southern
Cross.*

Half-an-hour passed before the door of Dan's
cabin was opened again, and Captain Bonhomme,
attended by the faithful Jean, reappeared. In the
skipper's hand was a pair of irons.

. "Monsieur," said the captain, holding up the
irons, "Madame de la Fontaine does you the
honour of desiring an interview in the saloon. May
I venture to enquire your pleasure?"

The ignominy of appearing before his charming
acquaintance of the day before manacled like a
criminal, was too much for Dan's vanity. "I give
you my word of honour," he said gruffly.

"Ah, monsieur," murmured the captain, "permit me to applaud your good taste. But let us be

exact: until you are returned to this cabin and are again under lock and key, that is to say until Madame is safely upon shore again,—you give me your word of honour as a gentleman to make no attempt to escape?"

"Yes, yes," said Dan, striving to conceal his irritation. "But spare me, I beg, your explanations. As you know, I am practically helpless. We understand each other. I trust that Madame de la Fontaine will give me an explanation of the outrage that you have refused."

"*Sans doute, sans doute!*" exclaimed the captain. He waved his hand toward the door. "*Aprés vous, monsieur.* Our worthy Jean will lead the way."

Without more ado they left the little cabin that had served as Dan's prison and traversed a narrow passageway aft to the door of a little saloon.

In the saloon, seated in a deep arm chair by the side of the table, was Madame de la Fontaine. She was clad in some soft green gown, with furs about her neck and wrists, and a little bonnet, adorned by the gay plumage of a tropical bird, worn close upon her head. At first glance she was as bewitchingly beautiful, as entirely charming, as she had seemed to Dan the day before. He blushed to the roots of his hair and for the moment quite forgot the extraordinary predicament in which he was placed. Madame de la Fontaine rose, a bright smile beaming from her soft blue eyes, and waited for Dan to approach.

"Good morning, Mr. Frost. This is charming of you. And now, Captain Bonhomme, if you will be so kind,—" she turned with her delightful smile to the skipper. "*Eh bien,* Jean!" This last remark was uttered in a sharp tone of command, very different from the silvery accents in which she had spoken to Frost and the captain. Dan wondered at it.

The disagreeable impression was but momentary, for the lady turned again to Dan, engaged him with her frank and pleasant glance, and young Frost forgot everything in the presence of the most charming woman he had ever met.

Captain Bonhomme and his watchdog had disappeared, closing the saloon door behind them. Dan and Madame de la Fontaine were alone.

"Will you not seat yourself, monsieur?" she said. "We shall then talk so much more at our ease."

"Thank you," Dan murmured vaguely, and advancing a step or two nearer, seated himself in the first chair within reach.

"Ah, not there, Mr. Frost," the lady protested with a little laugh of amusement. "It will never be that we are able to talk at so great a distance." She indicated a more comfortable chair at much closer quarters.

Dan obediently changed his seat, and waited for Madame de la Fontaine to begin the conversation. But she continued for a moment silently to regard him with a naïve air of interest and of unconcealed admiration.

"May I ask," said Dan at length, disturbed by this scrutiny, and rising to a courtesy that was in reality beyond him, "for what reason you have done me the honour to wish to speak with me?"

"*Vraiment*," replied Madame de la Fontaine; "after the events of last night there is need that we should have some conversation. You are very young and I have reason to be grateful to you for courtesy and kindness, so I have yielded to impulse, against my judgment, to interfere with Captain Bonhomme who has great anger with you."

"You are very kind, madame," Dan replied with dignity. "I am to infer then that my liberty or my further unwarranted imprisonment on this ship is to be determined by you?"

"*Mais non, Monsieur.* It is true only that I have a little influence with Captain Bonhomme. Last night you were watching me, so it interests me to know why."

"I was watching Mrs. Meath's house," Dan answered.

"Ah! but I and my maid were alone in the room into which you so unceremoniously looked, monsieur!"

"Yes, madame, but why should you infer that my motive in looking into that room was interest in your affairs?"

"I do not altogether assume that, Mr. Frost," the lady protested. "I infer simply—but, pardon! you were to say—?"

"Merely to ask you, madame, what Captain Bonhomme proposes to do with me, should you not be so good as to use your influence in my behalf?"

For reply the lady shrugged her shoulders a trifle. "I have fear, monsieur," she said after a moment, "that Captain Bonhomme will take you for a sail, perhaps a long sail, on the *Southern Cross.*"

"Then," said Dan, "since there is no doubt in my mind of your influence with the captain, I beg that you will have him release me."

"It is that that I desire, monsieur; and yet—?" Madame de la Fontaine paused and glanced at her companion with a charming little air of interrogation.

"And yet?" repeated Dan, flushing a little as he looked into the lovely blue eyes that met his so frankly.

"I confess, monsieur, I must first discover if you are really deserving of my efforts. I care to know very much why you watched me last night at the House on the Dunes. For what reason do you watch me at midnight? a stranger, a woman? Why is it that my affairs give you interest? I would know."

Her voice, her countenance expressed now only her sense of injury, an injury which, as it were, she was striving not to regard also as an insult. Under the persistent searching of her soft glance, Dan felt himself very small indeed.

"Answer me, if you please," she said. This time Dan detected just a trace of the sharpness with which she had dismissed the obsequious Jean. It gave him courage and a sense of protection from

the fascination he knew that this strange woman
was successfully exerting over him.

As he replied, his glance encountered hers with
frankness. "Madame de la Fontaine, I told you
yesterday morning, my sister, Nancy Frost, has
disappeared. We searched for her all day in vain.
Not a trace of her has been found. But certain
strange events have led me to suspect that certain
persons have had something to do with her disappearance and must know her whereabouts. I
will be frank Madame. One of the persons whom
I so suspect is yourself."

"I!—*mon Dieu!* and why is it that you believe
this, Monsieur?"

"I suspect you, madame, because I suspect the
Marquis de Boisdhyver."

"Ah! the French gentleman who is staying with
you at the Inn at the Red Oak, is it not so?"

"Yes."

"But—why me?"

"Because, madame, I discovered that you and
the Marquis de Boisdhyver have been in secret
communication with each other."

"*C'est impossible. Te me comprende pas, monsieur.* Will you tell me why it is that you can

think that this Marquis de Bois— what is the name?"

"De Boisdhyver."

"*Merci.* Why is it that you can think that the Marquis de Boisdhyver and I have been in secret communication?"

"Lights, green and red lights, have been used as signals;by the Marquis at the Inn; by you, madame, from the House on the Dunes; and by some one,—Captain Bonhomme, I suppose,—from this ship."

"Lights, you have seen lights?"

"Several times last night, Madame. My suspicions were aroused. I was determined to find my sister. I resolved to learn the meaning of those mysterious signals. My method was stupid: I blundered, and as you have several times so gently hinted, I am in your power."

For a moment Madame de la Fontaine was silent, then she looked quickly up; a half-vexed, half-amused expression curling her pretty lips.

"Look at me, monsieur," she said. "Do you know what you tell me? That I am an adventuress?"

Dan flushed suddenly as he met her steadfast gaze. "I have stated only a suspicion, madame, to

account for my own stupid blundering. But if
you think that my suspicions are extraordinary,
don't you think that our present situation and
conversation are also extraordinary, and that they
might rather confirm my suspicions?"

Madame de la Fontaine dropped her eyes with
a perceptible frown of displeasure; but again she
looked up, smiling.

"*C'est drole*, monsieur, but I find you very attractive? You are at once so naive and so clever?"

Dan, finding nothing to reply to this unexpected
remark, bit his lips.

"Will you not trust me?" she asked him suddenly, and putting out her hand she touched his
own with the tips of her fingers.

Poor Frost tingled at this unaccustomed contact. "I—I—" he stammered awkwardly. "I
have certainly no desire to distrust you, madame."

"And yet it is that you do distrust me."

"But what would you have me do?"

"Ah!" Her hand spontaneously closed upon his
with a clasp that delighted and yet disconcerted
him. "I hope that we shall make each other to
understand."

"What would you have me do?" Dan repeated.

"Monsieur, let me make to you a confession, I

understand your suspicions; I understand your desire to find if they are true. You have reason;
Monsieur le Marquis de Boisdhyver and I have
exchanged the mysterious signals that you have
witnessed. Why should I deny that which already
you know? Monsieur de Boisdhyver and I are
occupied with affairs of great importance, and it is
necessary that all is kept secret. But I believe,
that it is that I can trust you, monsieur."

"And Nancy—?" exclaimed Dan.

"Pas si vite, pas si vite!" said the lady, laugh-
ing gayly, Dan's hand still in her friendly pressure.
"All in good time, *mon ami.*" It is necessary before I confide in you our little secret that I consult
Monsieur le Marquis."

Dan's face betrayed his disappointment. "But
you do know about Nancy," he insisted; "you will
assure me—."

"Of nothing, dear boy,"—and she withdrew her
hand. "But it had been so much better for us all
if only Monsieur le Marquis had at the first con-
fided in you."

Madame de la Fontaine had risen now and was
holding out her hand to say good-bye.

"It is necessary that I return to the shore. I

will see Monsieur le Marquis this afternoon, and immediately afterward—"

"But, madame, surely," Dan exclaimed, "I am to accompany you?"

"Ah! monsieur," she replied with a charming little smile, "for the present you must rest content to be *mon captif*. We must quite clearly understand each other before—well. But you are too impetuous, Monsieur Dan. For the moment I leave you here."

"But Madame de la Fontaine," cried Dan, "I cannot consent—"

"No! no!" she said, as with a gay laugh, she placed a cool little hand across his mouth to prevent his finishing his sentence.

What absurd impulse fired his blood at this sudden familiarity, Dan did not know; but, quite spontaneously, as though all his life he had been in the habit of paying such gallantries to charming ladies, he kissed the soft fingers upon his lips. Madame de la Fontaine quickly withdrew them.

"Ah, *mon ami;*" she said, "I expected not to find here *une telle galanterie.*"

"I have offended you," murmured Dan, blushing furiously.

"Ah, *pas du tout!*" said Madame de la Fontaine. "You are a dear boy, monsieur Dan, and I —well, I find you charming."

As she said this, to Dan's complete confusion, Madame de la Fontaine lightly brushed his cheeks with her lips, and passing him rapdily, went out of the door of the saloon.

CHAPTER XII

TOM TURNS THE TABLES

Owing to his long watch during the greater part of the night, Pembroke slept heavily until late the next morning. Indeed, he did not waken until Jesse, alarmed that neither Dan nor he had appeared, knocked on their door. He sprang up quickly then, and began to dress hastily. Dan's bed had not been slept in, and Tom wondered how the night had gone with him.

In a few moments he was down stairs and in the breakfast-room. He found the Marquis de Boisdhyver already at table, pouring out his coffee, which Deborah had just placed before him. Mrs. Frost had not appeared.

Tom murmured an apology for being late, and delayed the black woman, who was on the point of leaving the room, by a question.

"Where is Mr. Dan?"

"Sure an, Mass' Tom, I ain't seen him dis mornin' yet. Ain't he done over-slept hisself like you?"

"No; but I dare say he is about the place some-wheres. All right, Deb; bring my breakfast quick-ly, please."

"You will pardon me," said Monsieur de Bois-dhyver, "for having begun without you?"

"Oh, certainly," said Tom; "Don't know what was the matter, but I slept unusually soundly last night; that is, after I got to sleep, for the storm kept me awake for hours."

"*Et moi anssi*," said the Marquis. "What wind! I am but thankful it has exhausted itself at last. And Monsieur Frost, he has also over-slept, you say?"

"No. He got up early without disturbing me. I guess he will be in any minute now."

The Marquis stirred his coffee and slowly sipped it.

Tom made a hasty breakfast, and then went outside to reconnoitre. He discovered no trace of his friend. There was but one inference in his un-easy mind: Dan had met with some misadventure at the House on the Dunes. At last, after wander-ing about aimlessly for some time, he decided to tell Jesse of his uneasiness.

"If Mr. Dan is not back by dinner time, I shall go over to the House on the Dunes and try to find out what has become of him. Heaven knows what has become of Miss Nancy. I don't like that schooner, Jess, and its ugly crew, lying there in the Cove. It's all a darn queer business."

"They're certainly a rough-looking lot, Mr. Tom, as I saw when I was on the beach yesterday. And she don't appear to have any particular business anchoring there. I hope they've nothing to do with Miss Nancy's and Mr. Dan's being away."

"I don't know, Jess, what to think, But listen here I want you to go into the Port this morning and engage Ezra Manners to come out here and stay with us for a week or so. Don't tell him too much, but I guess Ezra won't balk at the notion of a scrap. Bring him out with you, and offer to pay him enough to make sure of his coming. And I want you to go to Breeze's on the Parade and get some guns and powder, enough to arm every blessed soul of us in the Inn. Charge the stuff to me. And be careful how you bring it back, for I don't want any one here to know about it, particularly the old Frenchman. Understand? You ought to get back by dinner-time, if you start at once. I'll stay here till you return."

"I'll start right off, sir. Guess I'll have to drive,

for the rain 'll have washed the snow off the roads. I'll be back by halfpast twelve, Mr. Tom."

"All right," said Pembroke. "Be sure not to let any one now what you are doing."

"Sure I won't, sir. I've been pretty much worried myself about Miss Nancy. Didn't seem a bit like Miss Nance to go off without sayin' a word to anybody.

"Well, hurry along now, Jesse."

"Yes, sir."

Tom's next task was to try to explain to Mrs. Frost without alarming her. She happily jumped to the idea that Dan had gotten trace of Nancy, had gone to fetch her, and would return with her before nightfall. So Tom left her quite cheerfully knitting in her room for the day.

From time to time during the morning Tom wandered into the bar always to find Monsieur de Boisdhyver absorbed in his writing before the fire. The morning passed—a long restless morning for Pembroke—and nothing had happened. Dan had not returned. He tried to think out a plan of action. He went into the north wing of the Inn and barricaded the door leading from the bowling alley into the hallway. He made sure that all other doors and windows were fastened, and he put the key of the door that opened from the bar into the old wing into his pocket. Then he looked at the doors and windows in the south wing.

About noon, as he was standing at an upper window anxiously scanning the landscape for any sign of his friend, Tom saw the Marquis, wrapped in his great black cloak, emerge from the gallery, go down the steps by the Red Oak, and walk rapidly down the avenue of maples. He went along the Port Road, to the point where a little road branched off and led to the beach of the Cove; here he turned and walked in the direction of the beach. With the field glass Tom could follow him quite easily as he picked his way through the slush.

Beyond, on the waters of the Cove, the *Southern Cross* rode at anchor. A small boat had put off from the schooner, two seamen at the oars, and a woman seated in the stern. The boat reached the shore, the lady was lifted out upon the sands, the men jumped in again, pushed off and rowed briskly back to the schooner. Tom could not distinguish the lady's features, but from the style of her dress, cut in so different a fashion than that the ladies of Caesarea were wont to display, and from the character of her easy graceful walk, he judged that that was the Madame de la Fontaine, of whom Dan had told him the day before. The lady, whoever she might be, advanced along the beach and turned into the road down which the Marquis de Boisdhyver was going to meet her. Tom could see her extend her hand, and the old gentleman, bending ceremoniously, lift it to his lips. Then leaning against a stone wall beside a meadow of bedraggled snow, they engaged in animated conversation. The lady talked, the Marquis talked. They shrugged their shoulders, they nodded their heads, they pointed this way and then that. Poor Tom felt he must know what was being said. At last, their conference ended, they parted as ceremoniously as they had met, the lady starting across the Dunes and the Marquis retracing his steps toward the Inn.

In the meantime, fortunately before the Marquis reached the Port Road, Jesse had returned, accompanied by the able-bodied Ezra Manners, and laden with the supply of arms and ammunition that Pembroke had ordered.

Within half-an-hour Tom and Monsieur de Boisdhyver were seated together in the dining-room.

"Ah, and where is Monsieur Dan?" asked the

Marquis, with an affectation of cheerfulness. "Is he not returned?"

"Not yet, monsieur," Tom replied grimly.

"But you have heard from him?"

"Oh, yes," was Tom's answer; "I have heard from him of course."

"And from Mademoiselle Nancy, I trust, also?"

"Yes, from Nancy also."

"Ah, I am so relieved, Monsieur Pembroke. I was most anxious for their safety. One knows not what may happen. We shall have a charming little reunion at supper, *n'est-ce pas?*"

"Delightful," said Tom, but in a tone of voice that did not encourage the Marquis to ask further questions or to continue his comments.

After dinner, Tom slipped the field glass beneath his jacket, and ran upstairs to take another view of the countryside. To his great satisfaction he saw a dark spot moving across the snowy dunes and recognized the lady of the morning. Apparently she was on her way to the Cove again.

He took a loaded pistol, ran down stairs, gave Jesse strict orders to keep his eye on the Marquis, saddled his horse, and galloped off madly for Mrs. Meath's house.

When he reached the gate of the farmhouse,

Tom hitched his horse to the fence, went rapidly up the little walk, and knocked boldly and loudly on the front door. Repeated and prolonged knocking brought no response. He tried the door and found it fastened. He walked about the house. Every window on the ground floor was tightly closed and barred. There was no sign of life. He knocked at the door of the kitchen, but with no result. He tried it, and found it also locked. Determined not to be thwarted in his effort to see Mrs. Meath, he kicked vigourously against the door with his great hob-nailed boots. Unsuccessful in this, he detached a rail from the top of the fence and used it against the door as a battering-ram. At the first crash of timbers, the sash of a window in the second story, directly above the kitchen, was thrown open, and a dark-eyed, dark-haired, excessively angry-looking, young woman thrust her head out.

"*Qui va la?*" she exclaimed.

"Well," said Tom, smiling a little in spite of himself, for the young woman was in a state of great indignation. "I want to see Mrs. Meath. I may say, I am determined to see Mrs. Meath."

"*Peste! Je ne parle pas anglais!*" snapped the damsel.

"Very well then, mademoiselle, I'll try you in French," said Tom. And in very bad French indeed, scarcely even the French of Dr. Watson's school for the sons of gentlemen, Pembroke repeated his remarks.

"*Je ne comprend pas,*" said the young woman.

Tom essayed his explanation again, but whether the youthful female in the window could or would not understand, she kept repeating in the midst of his every sentence "*Je ne parle pas anglais,*" till Tom lost his temper.

"*Bien,* my fine girl," he exclaimed at last; "I am going to enter this house. If you won't open the door, I will batter it down. Understand? *Comprenez-vous?*"

"*Je ne parle pas anglais.*"

"As you will." He raised the fence-rail again and made as if to ram the door. "*Ouvrez la porte!* Do you understand that?"

"*Bete!*" cried the girl, withdrawing her head and slamming down the window.

Tom waited a moment to see if his threats had been effective, and was relieved by hearing the bar within removed and the key turned in the lock. The door was opened, and the young woman stood on the sill and volleyed forth a series of French

execrations that made Tom wince, though he did
not understand a word she was saying. Despite
her protests, he brushed her aside and stalked into the house. He went rapidly from room to room,
upstairs and down, from garret to cellar, the girl
following him with her chorus of abusive reproach.
She might have held her peace, thought Tom, for
within half-an-hour he was convinced that there
was not a person in the House on the Dunes save
himself and his excited companion. All he discovered for his pains was that old Mrs. Meith was
also among the missing.

"*Ou est Madame Meath?*"

"*Madame Meath! Que voulez vous? Je ne
connais pas Madame Meath....*" And infinitely
more of which Tom could gather neither head nor
tail.

Satisfied at last that there was nothing to be
gained by further search or parley with the
woman, he thanked her civilly enough and went
out. He unhitched his horse, vaulted into the
saddle, and dashed back, as fast as his beast could
be urged to carry him, to the Inn. He was certain now that the schooner held the secret of his
vanished friends, and it occured to him to play

their own game and turn the tables on Monsieur the Marquis de Boisdhyver.

Arrived at the Inn, Tom turned his horse, white with lather, over to Jesse; made sure that the Marquis was in the bar; and then, with the help of Manners, rapidly made a few preparations.

It was about five o'clock when, his arrangements completed, he returned to the bar, where Monsieur de Boisdhyver was quietly taking his tea. Tom bowed to the old gentleman, seated himself in a great chair about five feet away, and somewhat ostentatiously took from his pocket a pistol, laid it on the arm of his chair, and let his fingers lightly play upon the handle. The old marquis watched Pembroke's movements out of the corner of his eye, still somewhat deliberately sipping his tea. Manners, meanwhile, had entered, and stood respectfully in the doorway, oddly enough also with a pistol in his hand.

Suddenly Monsieur de Boisdhyver placed his teacup on the table, and leaning back in his chair, surveyed Tom with an air of indignant astonishment.

"Monsieur Pembroke," he said, "to what am I to attribute these so unusual attentions? Is it that you are mad?"

"You may attribute these unusual attentions, marquis, to the fact that from now on, you are not a guest of the Inn at the Red Oak, but a prisoner."

"Ah!" exclaimed the Marquis with a start, as he made a spasmodic motion toward the pocket of his coat. But if his intention had been to draw a weapon, Tom was too quick for him. The Marquis found himself staring into the barrel of a pistol and heard the unpleasant click of the trigger as it was cocked.

The old gentleman paled, whether with fright or indignation, Tom was not concerned to know. "You will please keep perfectly still, marquis."

"Monsieur Pembroke," exclaimed the old gentleman, "*C'est* abominable, outrageous, *Mon Dieu,* what insult!"

"Manners," said Tom, "kindly search that gentleman and put his firearms out of his reach."

"Monsieur, *c'est extraordinaire.* I protest."

"Quick, Ezra," replied Tom, "or one of us is likely to know how it feels to have a bullet in his skin. Up with your hands, marquis."

Monsieur de Boisdhyver obeyed perforce, while Manners quickly searched him, removed a small pistol from his coat pocket and a stiletto from his waistcoat, and handed them to Tom.

"I thought as much," said Pembroke, slipping them into his pocket. "Now, sir, you will oblige me by dropping that attitude of surprised indignation."

"Monsieur," said the Marquis, "What is it that you do? Why is it that you so insult me?"

"Monsieur, I will explain. You are my prisoner. I intend to lock you up safely and securely until my friend and his sister return, unharmed, to the Inn. When they are safe at home, when Madame de la Fontaine has taken her departure from the House on the Dunes, and when the *Southern Cross has* sailed out of the Strathsey, we shall release you and see you also safely out of this country. Is that clear?"

"*Mais, monsieur—*"

"I am quite convinced that you know where Nancy is and what has happened to Dan. As my friends are probably in your power or in the power of your friends, so, dear marquis, you are in mine. If you wish to regain your own liberty, you will have to see that they have theirs. Now kindly follow Manners; it will give him pleasure to show you to your apartment. There you may burn either red or green lights, and I am sure the snowbirds and rabbits of Lovel's Woods will enjoy them. After you, monsieur."

"Sir, I refuse."

"My dear marquis, do not make me add force to discourtesy. After you."

The Marquis bowed ironically, shrugged his shoulders, and followed Manners up the stairs. He was ushered into a chamber on the west side of the Inn, whose windows, had they not been heavily barred, would have given him a view but of the thick tangles of the Woods.

"I trust you will be able to make yourself comfortable here," said Tom. "Your meals will be served at the accustomed hours. I shall return myself in a short time, and perhaps by then you will have reconciled yourself to the insult I have offered you and be prepared to talk with me."

With that Tom bowed as ironically as the Marquis had done, went out and closed the door, and securely locked and barred it outside. Monsieur de Boisdhyver was left to his reflections.

CHAPTER XIII

For several hours after his return to the little cabin Dan had ample leisure in which to think over his extraordinary interview. There could be no doubt that the conspirators, for such he had come to call them to himself, were determined and desperate enough to go to any lengths in accomplishing their designs. Whether his suspicions and activity in seeking Nancy had precipitated their plans, his unexpected capture seemed to embarrass his captors as much as it did himself. At least, he gathered this from Madame de la Fontaine's conversation. Whatever might be the motive of the lady's proposed confidence, poor Frost could see nothing for it but to await their disclosure and then seize whatever advantage they might open to him. Notwithstanding the fact that Dan had cautioned himself against trusting the flattery of his charming visitor, notwithstanding that he told himself to be forewarned, even by his own suspicions, was to be forearmed, he was in

174

reality unconscious of the degree to which he had proved susceptible to the lady's blandishments, if indeed she had employed blandishments and had not merely given him the evidence of a good heart upon which his youth and naiveté had made a genuine impression.

Dan's experiences with girls up to this time had been limited. His emotional nature had never, as yet, been deeply stirred. But no one could be insensible to Madame de la Fontaine's beauty and charm, and her delightfully natural familiarity; and, finally, her fleeting kiss had seemed to Dan but evidence of a warm impulsive heart. To be sure, with all the good will in the world, he could not acquit her of being concerned in a mysterious plot—indeed, had she not admitted so much?—though, also, he must in justice remember that he knew very little of the nature of the plot in question.

As he paced restlessly back and forth the length of his prison, he tried to think clearly of the accumulating mystery. Was there a hidden treasure and how did the Marquis know about it? What part had the *Southern Cross* to play with its diabolical looking captain, and what could have become of Nancy? Then why had Madame de la

Fontaine—but again his cheek would burn and re-
membrance of the bewitching Frenchwoman blotted out all else.

At half-past twelve Captain Bonhomme appeared again. This time he invited Dan to par-
take of luncheon with him on the condition once
more of a parole. And Dan accepted. He and the
Captain made their luncheon together, attended
by the faithful Jean; and, though no mention was
made to their anomalous position, the meal was
not altogether a comfortable one. Captain Bonhomme asked a great many questions about the
country, to which Frost was inclined to give but
the briefest replies; nor, on his part, did he show
more disposition to be communicative in response
to Dan's questions about France. Jean regarded
the situation with obviously surly disapproval.
When the meal was finished, Frost was conducted
back to his little cabin.

About two o'clock he saw the small boat put off
for shore, and glancing in that direction, he was
relieved to see Madame de la Fontaine already
waiting upon the beach. Within half-an-hour he
was again in her presence in the Captain's saloon,
where their conversation had taken place in the
morning.

The lady received him graciously. "Ah! monsieur Dan, I fear you have had a weary day of it; but it was impossible for me to return sooner."

"It is very kind of you to return at all," replied Dan, gallantly enough.

"Now, Monsieur, you are anxious, I know, that I keep my promise of the morning."

"Most anxious," said Dan.

"Without doubt. Come here, my friend, sit near me and listen attentively to a long story."

"You have consulted with the Marquis?"

"*Mais oui.* It was difficult, but I have brought him to my way of thinking. I am certain that it was an error in the first place not taking you into our confidence. *Eh bien!* Tell me, do you know how your foster-sister came to be in the charge of your mother at the Inn at the Red Oak?"

"Yes, I know what my mother has told me. The child was abandoned to her rather than left in her charge."

"*Mais non,*" said Madame de la Fontaine; "General Pointelle was impelled to act as he did by the strongest motives,—nothing less than the tremendous task, undertaken for his country, to liberate the Emperor Napoleon from Elba. General Pointelle was a soldier,—more, he was a maréchal of the Empire; the greatest responsibilities devolved upon him. It was impossible for him to be burdened with a child."

"But why, madame, did he not take my mother into his confidence?"

"Secrecy was imperative, monsieur. Even to this day, you do not know who General Pointelle actually was. His was a name well-known in France, glorious in the annals of the Empire; a name, too, familiar to you in a somewhat different connection. 'General Pointelle' was the *nom-de-guerre*, as it were, of François, Marquis de Bois-dhyver, maréchal de France."

"François! you say, *François!*" exclaimed Dan.

"*Mais oui*, monsieur; but that should hardly astonish you so much as the fact that he was a Boisdhyver. Why are you surprised?"

"Simply, madame," exclaimed Dan hastily, "by the fact that it is the same name as that of our Marquis."

"Not quite," corrected the lady; "our Marquis —as you say—is Marie-Anne-Timeléon-Armand de Boisdhyver, the General's younger brother."

"Ah! and therefore Nancy's uncle?"

"Yes, the uncle of Nancy Frost, or of Eloise de Boisdhyver."

"I see," said Dan. "I begin to see."

"*Eh bien,* monsieur.   General Pointelle—the maréchal de Boisdhyver,—left the Inn at the Red Oak upon a mission for the Emperor, then at Elba. *Hélas!* that mission ended with disaster after the Hundred Days; for, as you know, the Emperor was sent in exile to St. Helena; and, as you may not know, the Maréchal de Boisdhyver was killed on the plains of Waterloo. *Allons;* when he left Deal, he concealed in a hidden chamber, which one enters, I believe, from a room you call the Oak Parlour, a large treasure, of jewels and gold.   This treasure, saved from the *debacle* in France, he had brought with him to America, and he hid it in the Inn, for the future of his little daughter Eloise. You remember that your mother was to hear something of advantage to her and the child, did not the General return.   It was the secret of the treasure and the directions to find it.   Well, Monsieur, at Waterloo, you must know, the Maréchal and his brother, the present Marquis, fought side by side.   François de Boisdhyver fell, nobly fighting for the glory of France; Marie-Anne had the good fortune to preserve his life, but was taken prisoner by the English.   Before the Maréchal received his death wound, the two brothers spoke with each other for the last time. In that moment, monsieur, the Marquis François revealed to the Marquis Marie-Anne that he had abandoned his daughter in America and that he had concealed in your old inn a treasure sufficient to provide for her future. He charged his brother to go to America, if he survived the battle; claim the little Eloise; rescue the treasure, and return with her to France and restore the fallen fortunes of the House of Boisdhyver.

"It took the Marquis Marie-Anne a long time to carry out his brother's dying injunctions," said Dan.

"Ah! but yes. You do not realize that the Marquis Marie-Anne, after the fall of Napoleon, spent many years in a military prison in England, for I have already told you that he fell into the hands of the enemy on the field of Waterloo. When at last he was released, he was aged, broken, and in poverty. His brother, in those dreadful moments on the battlefield, had been able to give him but the briefest description of the Inn at the Red Oak and the hidden treasure. He did not tell him where the treasure was, but only how he might obtain the paper of instructions which the Maréchal had concealed in a curiously-carved old cabinet in the Oak Parlour. The Maréchal, monsieur, loved the mysterious, and chose the device of tearing into two parts this paper of directions and concealing them in different hiding-places of the cabinet. Those directions, after many years, grew vague in the younger brother's memory.

"*Eh bien*, the Marquis was at last able to make the journey to this country. You must remember he had nothing wherewith to prove his story, if he gave you his confidence at once; and so, he decided to investigate quietly alone. But he won the confidence of Mademoiselle Nancy,—that is, of his niece, Eloise de Boisdhyver,—and revealed to her the secret of her identity and the mysterious story of the treasure. You follow me in all this, Monsieur Dan?"

"Perfectly, madame," Frost replied. "But as yet you have told me nothing of your own connection with this strange history."

"Pardon, dear boy," rejoined Madame de la Fontaine; "I was about to do so, but there is so much to tell. My own connection with the affair is quite simple. I am an old friend, one of the oldest, of Monsieur le Marquis de Boisdhyver, and, when I was a very young girl, I knew the Maréchal himself. It has been my happiness to be able to prove my friendship for a noble and a fallen family. One day last summer, Monsieur de Boisdhyver told me his brother's dying words, and it was I, Monsieur Dan, who was able to give the money for this strange expedition. The poor Marquis had lost quite all his fortune."

"I understand," said Frost. "But, yet, madame, I do not see the necessity for the secrecy, the mystery, for these strange signals at night, for these midnight investigations, for this schooner and its rough crew, for Nancy's disappearance, for my own imprisonment here."

"Please, please," murmured Madame de la Fontaine, as she held up her hands in smiling protest. "You go too fast for me. *Un moment, mon ami, un moment.* It was sixteen years ago that the Maréchal de Boisdhyver was a guest at the Inn at the Red Oak. You forget that the Marquis de Boisdhyver had no proof of his right to the treasure, save his own story, save his account of his brother's instructions on the field of Waterloo. By telling all he might have awakened deeper suspicions than by secrecy."

"That, I must say," Dan interrupted, "would hardly be possible."

"So!" exclaimed Madame de la Fontaine, with

an accent of displeasure. *"Ecoutez!* Monsieur le Marquis was to come a month in advance, as he did come; take up his quarters at the Inn; reconnoitre the ground; and win, if possible, the confidence and aid of mademoiselle.˙ He fortunately succeeded in this last, for he found it otherwise impossible to enter into the old wing of the Inn and examine the Oak Parlour. With the assistance of Eloise, this was accomplished at last, and the paper of directions was found; at least, found in part.

"Then I, having impressed the services of Captain Bonhomme and his ship the *Southern Cross,* set sail and arrived at the House on the Dunes only a few days ago, as you already know. The signals that you saw flashing at night were to indicate that all was well."

"The green light, I suppose," commented Dan, "was to indicate that; and the red—"

"Was the signal of danger. Because the Marquis discovered last night that you were not in the house; he flashed the warning that made Captain Bonhomme go to the House on the Dunes. Quite recently the manners of your friend, Mr.—eh—?"

"Pembroke?"

"Yes, Mr. Pembroke—led the Marquis to believe that he was being watched.

"I understand," said Dan, "but nothing you have told me so far, madame, accounts for Nancy's disappearance, and I am as anxious as ever to know where she is."

"Mademoiselle is perfectly safe, Monsieur Dan; I assure you. She left the Inn because she had fear of betraying our plans, particularly as she loved your friend, Mr. Pembroke."

"It is still strange to me, madame, that Nancy should distrust her oldest and best friends. But now you will let me see her?"

"Of course I shall soon, very soon, my dear boy. I have told you all, and now you will aid me to find the treasure that is your foster-sister's heritage, will you not?"

"Why certainly I want Nancy to have what is hers," replied Dan.

"Bravo, my friend. We are to count you one of us, I am sure."

"Just a moment," said Dan, resisting the temptation to touch the little hand that had been placed inpulsively upon his arm. "May I ask one more question?"

"A thousand, my dear, if you desire."

"Why then, since until last night everything has gone as you planned it, why has not the treasure already been discovered?"

"Because, *mon ami;* the Marquis has only been able to visit the Oak Parlour at night. And also it was decided to wait until I arrived."

"With the schooner?" suggested Dan.

"With the schooner, if you will. And you may remember that it was only the day before yesterday that I reached your so hospitable countryside."

"Ah! I understand; so then all that you desire of me, madame, is that I shall permit the Marquis or anyone else whom you may select for the purpose, to make such investigation of the Oak Parlour as is desired."

"Yes, my friend; and also there is yet another thing that we desire."

"But suppose, madame, that I cannot agree to that?"

Ah! *cher ami,* but you will. I confess—you must remember that the Marquis de Boisdhyver has been a soldier—that my friends have not agreed with me entirely. It has seemed to them simpler that we should keep you a prisoner on this ship, as we could so easily do, until our mission is accomplished. But,—I like you too much to agree to that."

Dan flushed a trifle, but he was not yet quite sure enough to fall in entirely with his charming gaoler's suggestions. "Madame de la Fontaine," he said after a moment's reflection, "I am greatly obliged to you for explaining the situation to me so fully. I shall be only too happy to help you, particularly in anything that is for the benefit of Nancy."

"I was sure of it. Now, my friend, there is a service that you can immediately render."

"And that is?" asked Dan.

"To entrust to me the other half of the paper of directions written by François de Boisdhyver, which you found in a secret cubby-hole in the old cabinet."

"What makes you think that I was successful in finding that, when the Marquis failed?"

"Because, at first having forgotten his precise directions after so many years, the Marquis could not find the fourth and last hiding-place in the cabinet, in which he knew the Maréchal had placed the other half of the torn scrap of paper. Another time he did find the cubby-hole, and it was empty. So knowing he was watched by you and Mr. Pembroke, he decided that you must have found it.   Is it not so, that you have it?"

"It is certainly not in my possession at this moment," said Dan.

"No, but you have it?"

"And if I have?"

"It is necessary for our success."

"Then, my first service, is to put you into complete possession of the secret?"

"If you will so express it."

"Very well, madame, I will do so; but, on one condition."

"And what is that, my friend?"

"That I be allowed to see Nancy, and that she herself shall ask me to do as you desire."

For a moment Madame de la Fontaine was silent.   *"Eh bien,"* she said at last, "you do not trust me?"

"But, dear madame, think of my situation, it is hard for me."

"Ah! I know it, believe me.   *C'est difficile.*   But I hoped you would trust me as I have you."

"Indeed, madame," exclaimed Dan, "I must try to think of everything, the mystery, this extraordinary mission upon which you are engaged, the fact that I am quite literally your prisoner.   When

I think about you, I know only you are beautiful, that you are lovely, and that I am happy near you."

She looked at him for a moment with a glance of anxious interrogation, as if to ask were it safe for her to believe these protestations. "You say, my friend," she asked at length, "that you care a little for me, for just me? *C'est impossible.* If Claire de la Fontaine could believe that, understand me, monsieur, it would be very sweet and very precious to her."

"I do care," cried Dan.

"Ah!" she exclaimed. "You have touched my heart. I am not a young girl, *mon ami*, but I confess that you have made me to know again the dreams of youth."

"Only let me prove that I care," cried Dan, considering but little now to what he committed himself.

"Let me prove," cried she, "that I too believe in you. I must first see the Marquis, and then, to-night, if it can be arranged, you shall receive from Eloise de Boisdhyver's own lips the request I have made of you. But if, for any reason, this cannot be arranged for to-night, you must be patient till morning; you must trust me to the extent of remaining on this ship. I cannot act entirely on my own judgment, but I assure you that in the end my judgment will prevail. And now, *au revoir.*"

She placed her hand in his, and responded to the impulsive pressure with which he clasped it. Their eyes met; in Dan's the frankest expression of her conquest of his emotions; in her's a glance at once tender and sad, above all a glance that seemed to search his spirit for assurance that he was in earnest. Suddenly fired by her alluring beauty, Dan drew her to him and bent his head to hers.

"Ah! my friend," she murmured, "you are taking an unfair advantage of the fact that this morning I too rashly yielded to an impulse."

"I cannot help it," Dan stammered. "You bewitch me." He bent lower to kiss her cheek, when he suddenly thrilled to the realization that his lips had met hers.

A moment later Madame de la Fontaine was gone and Captain Bonhomme had reappeared in the doorway.

CHAPTER XIV

Tom Pembroke was as good as his word. He returned to the little room, in which he had confined the Marquis, within an hour after he had left him. It was then nearly supper-time and dusk was fast settling upon the gloomy countryside. An unwonted calm had fallen upon land and sea after the sharp blow of the previous night, but the sky was still gray and there was promise of more rain, if not of wind.

To Tom's indignation and alarm, though scarcely to his surprise ,there had been no sign or word from Dan or Nancy. Shortly after he had left the Marquis, he saw, by aid of the field-glass, Madame de la Fontaine, attended by two seamen, leave the schooner and return to the House on the Dunes. He smiled a little as he thought of the account the lively young maid-servant would give of his recent visit. But withal, he felt very much as if he were playing a game of blind man's buff and that he was "it." He was impatient for his interview with the Marquis, though he was but little hopeful that an hour's confinement would have been sufficient to bring the old gentleman to terms. Nor was he to be surprised.

He found Monsieur de Boisdhyver huddled in a great arm chair near the fire that that been kindled on the hearth of his prison. The Marquis glanced up, as Tom entered, but dropped his eyes at once and offered him no greeting. Tom placed his candle on the table and, drawing up a chair, seated himself between the Marquis and the door.

"Well, sir," he said at last, "as I promised you, I have returned within an hour. Have you anything to say to me?"

"Have I anything to say to you!" exclaimed the Marquis. "For why, monsieur? If I venture to express my astonishment and indignation at the way I am treated, you subject me to a barbarity that could be matched no where else in the civilized world than in this extraordinary country. My life is menaced with firearms. My protests are sneered at. I have left but one inference—you have gone mad."

"No, marquis," said Pembroke, "I am not mad. I am simply determined that the mysteries by which we have been surrounded and of which you

are the center, shall cease. You have a free choice:
put me in the way of getting my friend and his
sister back to the Inn, or resign yourself to a prolonged confinement in this room."

"But monsieur I have nothing to communicate
to you concerning the disappearance of your
friends."

"Pardon me, marquis," returned Pembroke;
"you have much to communicate to me. Perhaps
you are not aware that I know the motive of your
coming to the Inn at the Red Oak; that I know
the reason for your prolonged stay here; that I
know of the influence that you have acquired over
Nancy Frost; and that I have been a witness of
your midnight prowlings about the Inn. Nor am
I in ignorance of your connection with the rascal-
ly-looking captain of the schooner at anchor in the
Cove and with the mysterious woman, who has
taken possession of the House on the Dunes. I
am convinced that you know what has become of
Dan as well as what has happened to Nancy. And,
believe me, I am determined to find out."

"*Bein!*" exclaimed Monsieur de Boisdhyver,
"permit me to wish you good luck in your undertaking. I repeat, Monsieur Pembroke, I have no
information to give to you. I do not know to

what extent I have been watched, but I may say with truth that my actions do not in the least concern you."

"They concern my friends," said Tom. "Dan, as you know, is more to me than a brother; and as for his sister Nancy, I hope and expect to make her my wife."

"In that case," rejoined the Marquis with ill-concealed irony, "I may be permitted to offer to you my congratulations. But even so, monsieur, there is nothing that I can do to facilitate your matrimonial plans."

"You refuse then to come to terms?" asked Pembroke.

The Marquis raised his hands with a gesture of despair. "What shall I say, monsieur? If you insisted upon my flying from here to yonder beach, I might have all the desire in the world to oblige you, but the fact would remain that I was without the means of doing so. Since you are so little disposed to accept my protestations, I will no longer make them, but simply decline your proposal. And, pardon me, but so long as I am submitted to the indignity of this confinement, it would be a courtesy that I should appreciate if you would spare me your company."

"Very good," said Tom. "Your meals will be served regularly; and you may ask the servant for anything necessary. I shall not visit you again until you request me to do so."

"*Merci,*" said the Marquis drily. He rose from his seat as Dan turned toward the door, and bowed ironically.

Pembroke went downstairs to have his supper with Mrs. Frost. He said what he could to pacify her, not altogether with success, for as darkness fell the old lady became increasingly apprehensive.

"I know you are anxious, Mrs. Frost," said Tom, "but you must not worry. Try to believe that all will come out right. I am going out after supper, but I shall leave Jesse and Ezra on guard, and you may be sure everything will be safe."

It was some time before Mrs. Frost would consent to his leaving the Inn. If she had yielded to her inclinations, she would have spent the evening in hysterics with Tom at hand to administer comfort. Pembroke, however, deputed that office to black Deborah, and immediately after supper set about his business.

He gave the necessary instructions to Jesse, Ezra and the maids, saw that everything was closely locked and barred, supplied himself with arms and ammunition, and slipped out into the night. Having saddled Fleetwing, he swung himself on the young hunter's back, and trotted down the avenue to the Port Road. The night was intensely dark and still. The moon had not yet risen, and a thick fog rolled in from the sea, shrouding the countryside with its impenatrable veil.

At the Beach Road Pembroke dismounted, tied his horse to a fence rail, and proceeded thence on foot toward the Cove. Stumbling along through the heavy sand, he made his way to the boathouse at the northern end of the little beach. There he ventured to light his lantern, unlocked the door and stepped within. On either side of the entrance were the two sailboats that he and Dan used in summer and to the rear was the old-fashioned whaleboat with which they did their deep fishing. Over it, in a rudely constructed rack, was the Indian birch-bark canoe which Dan had purchased in the mountains a few years before. As the sea had fallen to a dead calm, he decided to use this canoe, which he could paddle quite noiselessly, and pulling down the little craft from its winter resting-place, he carried it to the water's edge. The sea, so angry the night before, now scarcely murmured; only a low lazy swell, at regularly recurring inter-

vals, slapped the shore and hissed upon the sands.
Tom pushed the nose of the canoe into the water,
leaped lightly over the rail, and with his paddle
thrust it off the beach. He was launched without
mishap.

Not the faintest gleam of light showed the position of the *Southern Cross,* but estimating as well
as he could the general direction, he paddled out
through the enshrouding fog. For ten minutes or
so, he pushed on into the strange, misty night.
Then suddenly he found himself alongside an old
fisherman's yawl that had been rotting all winter
at her moorings, and he knew from her position
that he could not be far from the *Southern Cross.*

A few more strokes to leeward, and a spot of
dull light broke through the darkness. He headed
directly for it. To his relief it grew brighter;
when suddenly, too late to stop the progress of his
canoe, he shot under it, and the bow of his craft
bumped with a dull thud against the timber side
of the schooner. Its dark outlines were just perceptible above him; and at one or two points there
gleamed rays of light in the fog, green and red
from the night lamps on the masthead, and dull
yellow from the port holes in the rear. A second
after the contact the canoe receded, then the wash

of the sea drew her toward the stern. Another
moment and Pembroke felt his prow scrape gently
against the rudder, which prevented further drift-
ing. Apparently, since he heard nothing from the
deck above, he had reached his goal without at-
tracting attention.

He kept perfectly still, however, for some little
time, until satisfied that there was no one at the
wheel above, he pushed the canoe softly back to
the rope ladder, that a day or so before he had
seen hanging over the side. It was the work of a
moment to make his little boat fast to the lower
rung. Then slipping over the rail, he climbed
stealthily up till his head protruded above the
gunwhale. The immediate deck seemed deserted;
but he was sure that some one was keeping the
watch, and probably near the point where he was,
that is to say, where access to the deck was easiest.
But the fog and the darkness afforded him protection, as he climbed over the gunwhale and, without making a sound, moved toward the stern,
crossed the after-deck and found the wheel. As
he had surmised, it was deserted. The watch evidently was forward. Beneath him, sending its in-
effectual rays obliquely into the fog, shone the
light from the little cabin below.

Determined to get a look through the port, he climbed over the gunwhale again, fastened a stern-sheet about his waist and to a staple, and at the risk, if he slipped or if the rope gave way, of plunging head foremost into the icy waters of the Cove, he let himself down until his head was on a level of the port.

Through the blurred glass he peered into a tiny cabin. There with back toward him, just a few feet away stood Nancy Frost. He steadied himself with an effort, and looking again saw that she was alone. A moment's hesitation, and he tapped resolutely on the pane with his finger tips. At first Nancy did not hear, but presently, aroused by the slight tapping, she glanced with a frightened expression toward the door, and stood anxiously listening. Tom continued to knock on the window, not daring to make it louder for fear of being heard above. The alarm deepened on Nancy's face, and in sheer pity Tom was tempted to desist; but at that instant her attention was riveted upon the spot whence the tapping came. At last, still with the expression of alarm on her face, she came slowly toward the port. She hesitated, then pressed her face against the pane over which Tom had spread his fingers. At whatever risk, of frightening her or of danger to himself, as she drew back, he pressed his own face against the outside of the little window glass. She stared at him as if she were looking at a ghost.

He moved his lips to form the word "Open." At length, in obedience to this direction, Nancy cautiously unloosened the window of the port and drew it back.

"Good heavens, Tom!" she whispered. "Is it you?"

"Yes, yes," Pembroke whispered back. "But for God's sake, speak softly. I'm in a devilishly unpleasant position, and can hang here but a minute. Tell me quickly—are you here of your own free will or are you a prisoner?"

"How can you ask?" she exclaimed. "For the love of heaven, help me to escape."

"That's what I'm here for," was Toms reply. "Now, quick; are you only locked in or barred as well? I've brought some keys along."

"Only locked, I think."

"Where does that door lead?"

"Into a little passage off the companion-way. Give me your keys. They have but one man on watch. The captain is on shore to-night, apt to return at any moment. And you?"

"I have a canoe tied to the ladder on the shore side. If the captain returns, I'm caught. Try those keys." He slipped into her the bunch of keys that he had brought along. "I was sure you were here, and against your will."

"Dan, too, is locked up on board."

"I thought as much; but you first. Hurry."

Nancy sprang to the door, trying one key after another in feverish haste. At last, to Tom's infinite relief, he saw the key turn in the lock, and the door open.

"On deck," she whispered; "at the ladder. I'm not likely to be caught." Then she waved her hand and disappeared into the passage.

Tom pulled himself up, unloosed the rope, and stole along the rail toward the ladder. For a few moments, which seemed like a thousand years, he stood in anguished suspense waiting for Nancy. Then suddenly she came out of the mist and was at his side. They stood for a moment like disembodied spirits, creatures of the night and the fog. The next instant a hand shot out and grasped the girl's shoulder.

"*Peste! mam'zelle*," a rough voice hissed, "*ou allez-vous?*"

As the man spoke Tom swung at him with the

butt of his revolver, and without a murmur the figure fell to the deck.

"Quick now," Pembroke whispered, "down the ladder."

Instantly Nancy was over the rail and Tom was climbing down after her. As he knelt in the bow and fumbled with the painter, the plash of oars sounded a dozen yards away.

"*Ho! Croix du Midi!*" came a hail through the fog.

"Curse it!" muttered Tom; "the painter's caught." He drew out his knife, slashed the rope that bound them to the schooner, got to his place amidships, and pushed the canoe free. The lights of a small boat were just emerging from the dark a dozen feet away. But the canoe slid by unobserved, in the fog. They heard the nose of the small boat bump against the schooner; then an oath, and a man's voice calling the watch.

"They've found my painter," whispered Tom, "and in a second they'll find the sailor on their deck."

The lights of the *Southern Cross* grew dim; vanished; the sound of angry voices became muffled. They were half-way to shore when they heard the noise of oars again. Evidently some one had started in pursuit. For a moment Tom rested, listening intently; but the sound was still some distance away. Probably, he thought, they were heading directly for the shore, whereas he, at a considerable angle, was making for the boathouse at the north end of the beach. In ten minutes he had beached the canoe within a rod of the point from where he embarked.

"I can't hear them," whispered Tom, after a moment's listening. "They've made for shore down the beach. They can't find us in the dark. I've got Fleetwing tied to a fence in the meadow yonder. Come."

It was the work of a moment to stow the canoe, lock the boathouse, run across the sands, and mount Nancy in front of him on the back of his trusty hunter. A second later Fleetwing's hoofs were striking fire on the stones that the high tides had washed into the beach road. In the distance there was a cry, the sharp ring of a pistol shot; but they were safe on their way, racing wildly for the Inn. The escape, the adventure had thrilled Nancy. Tom's arms were around her, and her hands on his that grasped the bridle. At last they were in the avenue, and Tom pulled in under the great branches of the Red Oak. He slipped from the back of the horse and held out his arms to Nance.

"We are safe, girl," he whispered.

"You are sure? Oh, thank God, thank God! Quick, let us in! Can they be following?"

"No, no. They won't follow. It's all right. Easy,—before we go in—please, dear—once—kiss me."

"Oh, Tom, Tom," she whispered, as she lifted her face to his.

"I have you at last, sweetheart," he murmured. "You love me?"

"Ah!" she cried, "with my whole heart and soul."

CHAPTER XV

It was after eleven before Nancy rejoined Tom in the bar. She seemed more like herself as she slipped in and took her accustomed seat beside the blazing logs.

"Oh, I am all right, thank you," she insisted, declining the glass of wine that Pembroke poured out for her. "I wonder, Tom, if you killed that poor wretch on the deck?"

"Don't know," Tom answered. "I hope so. But what the deuce, Nance, has been happening? I can wait till to-morrow to hear, if you are too tired to tell me; but I do want awfully to know."

"I am not tired," Nancy replied, "and I shan't sleep a wink anyway. If I close my eyes I'll feel that hand on my shoulder and hear the thud of that man's fall on the deck. I can't bear to think that this miserable business will bring bloodshed."

"But tell me, Nance, who is the Marquis—what happened—how did they get you away?"

"Ah! the Marquis," exclaimed Nancy with a

204

shudder. "I am glad you have him locked up. I can't bear to think of him, but I'll tell you what I know. You remember, Tom, he tried to be friends with me from the first; and he seemed to fascinate me in some unaccountable way. Then he questioned me about my identity, an began to drop hints that he knew more than he cared to let appear to the others, and my curiosity was excited. I have always known of course that there was some mystery about my being left to Mrs. Frost's care. She has been kind, good, all that she should be; but she wasn't my mother. Well, the Marquis stirred all the old wonder that I had as a child, and before long quite won my confidence. He told me after a time that I was the daughter of his elder brother, the Marquis François de Boisdhyver, who in 1814 stayed here at the Inn at the Red Oak under the name of General Pointelle. I was not altogether surprised, for I have always believed that I was French by birth, and his assertion that I was his niece seemed to account for his interest in me. My father, if this Marquis de Boisdhyver was my father, was one of the Emperor Napoleon's marshals and was a party to the plot to rescue the Emperor from Elba. He was obliged to return to France, and since it was impossible for him to take me with him—I was a little girl of two at the time—he left me with Mrs. Frost. Thinking of my future, he hid a large treasure in some secret chamber off the Oak Parlour."

"I know," Tom interrupted.

"What? You mean there is a treasure?"

"I think there is; but go on. I will tell you afterwards."

"Then he set sail for France, took part in the great events of the Hundred Days, and fell at Waterloo. It was on the field of Waterloo that he met his younger brother—our Marquis—and told him about the child left in America and about the treasure hidden in the Inn at the Red Oak."

"Well," Nancy continued, having answered a volley of questions from Tom, "the Marquis—I mean our old Marquis—was held for many years in a military prison in England. Upon his release he was poor and unable to come to America to seek his little niece and the fortune that he believed to be hidden in the Inn. Tom, at first I didn't believe this strange story about a treasure; but gradually I became convinced; for the Marquis believed in it thoroughly, and for proof of it he showed me a torn scrap of paper that he found in the cabinet in the Oak Parlour the day after he arrived at the Inn. It seems the old marshal had torn the paper in two and hidden the parts in different cubbyholes of that old Dorsetshire cabinet. He couldn't find an opportunity to hunt for the other half, so at last he persuaded me to help him in the search. Of course, he swore me to secrecy, and I was foolish enough to give him my promise. I got the key to the bowling alley from the ring in Dan's closet, and two or three times went with him at night after you all were asleep."

"I know you did," said Tom.

"How could you know it—has the Marquis—?"

"No, Dan and I saw you. I woke one night, happened to look out of the window and saw the Marquis going into the bowling alley. It was moonlight, you know. I woke Dan, we slipped down stairs, saw a light in the Oak Parlour, peeped through the shutters and saw you and the old Marquis at the cabinet."

"When was this?" asked Nancy.

"The night—before our walk in the woods."

"And you did not tell me! What could you think I was doing?"

"I didn't know. How could I know? It was that which first made me suspicious of the Marquis. We made up our minds to watch. But that day in the woods—well, I forgot everything in the world but just that I was in love with you."

"Ah!" exclaimed Nancy, flushing.

"But tell me," asked Tom, "What did you find in the cabinet?"

"We found nothing. I began to think that the Marquis had deceived me. I didn't know what to believe. I didn't know what to do. I threatened each day to tell Dan. And then came our walk. When we came in that night—do you recall?— we found the Marquis sitting in the bar before the fire, and I went over and spoke to him."

"Yes, I remember," Tom answered.

"I had made up my mind that I must take you all,—mother and you and Dan,—into my confidence. I told him so. He begged me to wait until the next day and promised that he would tell you then himself. I was beginning to think he might be a little crazy, that there was no hidden treasure."

"I'm sure there is," said Tom. "There was another half of that torn scrap of paper, hidden in one of the cubbyholes of the old cabinet. Dan found it. It's the directions, sure enough, for finding the treasure."

"Ah! but what has it all to do with me?"

"I don't know; something I fancy, or the Marquis would not have told you as much as he did. But here is the other half. You can tell whether it is part of the paper he showed you."

He drew from his pocket the yellowed bit of paper and spread it on the table before them. Nance bent over and examined it closely.

"I believe it is the other half. See, it is signed ...'ançois de Boisdhyver'. I remember perfectly that the signature of the other was missing, except for the letters 'F-r-' It is, it must be, François de Boisdhyver, who, the Marquis says, was my father. Then look! here are the words 'trésor', 'bijoux et monaie'. I remember in the other there were phrases that seemed to go with these—'trésor caché' 'lingots d'or'. Ah! do you suppose there really is a fortune hidden away in the Inn all these years?"

"Yes, I think so," said Tom. "And I feel certain you have some claim to it, or they wouldn't have made such an effort to involve you in their plot. But, please, Nance, tell me the rest. You got to the night of your disappearance."

"It was a horror—that night!" exclaimed Nancy. "It must have been about twelve that the Marquis came and tapped at my door. For some reason I was restless and had not gone to bed. I slipped out into the hall with him and we came in here to talk. He begged me to make one more expedition with him to the Oak Parlour. But I refused—I insisted that I must tell Dan. Suddenly, Tom, without the slightest warning, I felt my arms pinioned from behind, and before I could scream, the Marquis himself had thrust a handkerchief in my mouth, and I was gagged and bound. Everything was done so quickly, so noiselessly, that not a soul in the house could have heard. They carried me out of the Inn and into the avenue of maples. From there on I was forced to walk. We went to the beach. I was put into a small boat and rowed out to the schooner, and there they locked me up in the little cabin in which you found me."

"What time did you say it was?" asked Tom.

"About twelve—after midnight, perhaps; I don't know for sure. The Marquis went to the beach with us and pretended to assure me that I was in no danger; that I would be released in good time, and that he would see me again. As a mat-

ter of fact for three days I have seen no one but
Captain Bonhomme. He brought my meals, and
was inclined to talk about anything that come into his head. Last night he told me that Dan was
also a prisoner on the *Southern Cross,* if that
would be of any consolation to me. Then he said
he had to go ashore and locked me up. Several
times I was taken on deck for exercise, but the
captain kept close by my side."

"And you haven't seen or heard from the Marquis again?"

"No! nor do I want to see him. But, Tom,
what is the meaning of it all? How are we going
to rescue Dan? What are we going to do? We
can't keep the Marquis a prisoner indefinitely."

Tom gave her his own version of the last few
days. He told her of what he and Dan had sus-
pected, of Dan's proposal to visit the House on the
Dunes and his disappearance, of his own investigations there, and his determination to play the
same game with the Marquis as hostage.

"But what to do next, I confess I don't know,"
he continued. "At present it seems to be stale
mate. For to-night, any way, we are safe, I think,
for I shall take turns in keeping guard with Jesse
and Ezra. I have the idea that to-morrow, when

they realize something has happened to the Marquis we shall hear from Madame de la Fontaine or from the schooner. In the morning I am going to take you and Mrs. Frost to the Red Farm for safety. I intend to fight this thing out with that gang, whatever happens. If there is treasure, according to their own story, it belongs to you. If I don't get a proposal from them, I shall make the offer, through Madame de la Fontaine, of exchanging the Marquis for Dan.... But I must go now, Nance, and relieve one of the men. We must all get some sleep to-night, and it's already after twelve. Go to bed, sweetheart, and try to get some rest. One of us will be within call all night, watching right there in the hall; so don't be afraid."

"It was my wretched curiosity that got us into all this trouble."

"Not a bit of it! The trouble was all arranged by the Marquis; he was simply waiting for the schooner. Now that I have you back again, my heart is fairly light. We shall get Dan to-morrow, I am sure."

CHAPTER XVI

In the morning the fog lifted, a bright sun shone from a cloudless sky, the marshes sparkled with pools of melted snow and the long-promised thaw seemed definitely to have set in. Soon after breakfast Tom sent Jesse to the Red Farm with directions for the people there to make preparations for Mrs. Frost and Nancy, whom he proposed to drive over himself in the course of the afternoon.

About the middle of the morning as Tom and Nancy stood on the gallery discussing the situation, Tom drew her attention to a small boat putting off from *The Southern Cross*. They examined it through the glass, and Nancy recognized the figure of Captain Bonhomme sitting amongst the stern-sheets.

"You may depend upon it," said Tom, "he is going to the House on the Dunes to report your disappearance to Madame de la Fontaine. The most curious thing about this whole business to me is the mixing-up in it of such a woman as Dan described Madame de la Fontaine to be."

"It is strange," Nancy agreed, "but from the bits of talk I've overheard, I should say that she was the prime mover in it all."

"In a way I am rather glad of that," said Tom, "for with a woman at the head of things there is less chance of their resorting to force to gain their ends. But the stake they are playing for must be a big one, and already they have done enough to make me sure that we should be prepared for anything. I shall be surprised if we don't get some communication from them to-day. The old Marquis counts on it, or he would not keep so still. At any cost, we must get Dan back."

They talked for some time longer and were about to go in, when Nancy pointed to a horse and rider coming down the avenue of Maples. A glance sufficed to show that the rider was a woman. Nancy slipped inside to escape observation, while Tom waited on the gallery to receive the visitor.

As the lady drew rein under the Red Oak, he ran down the steps, and helped her to dismount. Her grace, her beauty, her manner as of the great world, made him sure that he was in the presence of Madame de la Fontaine.

"Good morning, sir," said the lady, with a charming smile, "if I mistake not, I have the pleasure of addressing Mr. Pembroke?"

"Yes, madam,—at you service," replied Tom.

"I am come on a strange errand, monsieur; as an ambassadress, so to say, of those whom I fear you take to be your enemies."

"You are frank, madam. I believe that I am speaking with—?"

"Madame de la Fontaine," the lady instantly supplied. "Events have so precipitated themselves, monsieur, that pretense and conventionality were an affectation. I am informed, you understand, of your brilliant rescue of Mademoiselle Eloise de Boisdhyver."

"If you mean Nancy Frost by Mademoiselle Eloise de Boisdhyver, madam, your information is correct. I gathered that you had been told of this, when I saw Captain Bonhomme make his way to the House on the Dunes this morning."

"Ah! What eyes, monsieur!" exclaimed the lady. "But I have grown accustomed to having my privacy examined over-curiously during the few days I have spent on your hospitable shores. *Mais pardon*—my purpose in coming to the Inn at the Red Oak this morning was but to request that my name be conveyed to Monsieur the Marquis de Boisdhyver."

"You mean, madam, that you wish to see the Marquis?"

"Yes, monsieur, if you will be so good as to allow me to do so."

"I am sorry," Tom rejoined, "that I must disappoint you. Circumstances over which the Marquis has no control will deprive him of the pleasure of seeing you this morning."

"Ah!" exclaimed Madame de la Fontaine, "I was right then. Monsieur le Marquis is, shall we say, in confinement?"

"As you please, madam; as safe, for the time, as is my friend Dan Frost."

"*Eh bien*, monsieur! It is that you have—do you not say?—turned the tables upon us?"

"Precisely, madam," assented Tom.

"And you will not permit me even a word—ever so little a word—with my poor friend?" murmured Madame de la Fontaine plaintively.

"Again I am sorry to refuse you, madam; but—not even a little word."

"So! *Mais oui*, I am not greatly surprised. I was assured last night...."

"When you did not see the signals?" suggested Tom quickly.

"When I did not see the signals," repeated the lady, with a glance of the briefest enquiry, "I was assured that something had befallen Monsieur le Marquis. *Mais vraiment,* monsieur, you do as much dishonour in assuming a wicked conspiracy on our parts. The Marquis is my friend; he is also the friend of the charming Mademoiselle. All that we wish, all that we would do is as much in her interest as in his own. But it is impossible that my old friend shall remain in confinement. On what condition, monsieur, will you release the Marquis de Boisdhyver?"

"On the condition, naturally, that my friend Dan Frost is released from the *Southern Cross.*

"Ah! Is it that you are quite sure that Monsieur Frost is confined on the ship?"

"Quite sure, Madame de la Fontaine. I was on board *The Southern Cross* last night."

"Yes, I know it; and I congratulate you upon your extraordinary success. Very well, then, I accept your condition. Monsieur Dan Frost returns; Monsieur le Marquis is released. And now you will perhaps have the kindness—"

"No, madame; in this affair the Marquis and his

friends have been the aggressors. I cannot consent that you should hold any communication with the Marquis till Dan returns free and unharmed to the Inn."

"And what assurance then shall I have that the Marquis will be released?"

"None, madame, but my word of honour."

"*Pardon, monsieur.* I accept your terms. Monsieur Frost shall return. The instant he enters the Inn at the Red Oak, you promise that the Marquis de Boisdhyver be released and that he be given this note from me?"

"Certainly, madam."

The lady took a sealed note from the pocket of her habit and handed it to Tom. "There remains, monsieur," she murmured, "but to bid you good-day. If you will be so kind—"

She ran lightly down the steps, and held up her foot for Tom to assist her into the saddle.

"Your friend will return *tout de suite,* monsieur," she cried gayly, as she drew in the rein.

"And we shall have the pleasure of seeing you again?" asked Tom.

"Ah! who can tell?" She touched the horse lightly with her whip, inclined her head, and soon disappeared down the avenue of maples.

Some time later Nancy and Tom watched her cantering across the beach. She waved her handkerchief as a signal to the schooner; a small boat put ashore, and she was rowed out to *The Southern Cross.*

"Once Dan is back, and we get rid of the old Marquis," said Tom, "I shall breathe considerably easier."

"I can't believe they will give the game up so easily," was Nancy's reply. "Seizing the Marquis, Tom, was a check, not a mate."

Out on the schooner in the Cove, Madame de la Fontaine and Dan Frost were once more talking together.

"Dear boy," said the lady. "I cannot do that which I promised. It is impossible that your sister shall make to you the request to give me the torn scrap of paper, for the reason that Mademoiselle Nancy has chosen to disappear. Have no fear, monsieur, for I have good reason to believe she has returned to the Inn at the Red Oak. Our schemes, *mon ami,* have failed. You are no longer a prisoner, you are free. And this is good-bye. I abandon our mission. I leave the House on the Dunes to-day; to-morrow I return to France."

"But, madame, you bewilder me," exclaimed

Dan. "Why should you go; why should we not all join forces, hunt for the treasure together, if there is a treasure; why this division of interests?"

"*C'est impossible!*" she exclaimed impetuously. "Monsieur le Marquis will not consent. He is treated with intolerable rudeness by your friend Mr. Pembroke. He will not accept that which I propose. And I—*vraiment, I* desire no longer to work against you. No, monsieur Dan, *tout est fini*, we must say good-bye."

She held out her hands and Dan impetuously seized them. Then, suddenly, she was in his arms and his lips were seeking hers.

"I cannot let you go," he cried hoarsely. "I cannot say good-bye."

For a moment he held her, but soon, almost brusquely, she repulsed him. .."*C'est folie, mon ami, folie!* We lose our heads, we lose our hearts."

"But I love you," cried Dan. "You must believe it; will you believe it if I give you the paper?"

"No, no!—What!—you wish to give to me the secret of the Oak Parlour?—"

"Aye, to entrust to you my life, my soul, my honour."

"Ah, but you must go," she murmured tensely.

"Captain Bonhomme is returning. It is better that he knows of your release after you are gone. *C'est vrai*, my friend, that I risk not a little in your behalf. Go now, quickly... No! No!" she protested, as she drew away from him. "I tell you, *C'est folie*,—madness and folly. You do not know me. Go now, while there is time!"

"But you will see me again?" insisted Dan. "Promise me that; or, on my honour, I refuse to leave. Do with me what you will, but—"

"Listen!" she whispered hurriedly. "I shall meet you to-night at ten o'clock, at the end of the avenue of maples near to your inn; you know the place? *Bien!* Bring me the paper there, to prove that you trust me. And I—*mais non*, I implore you—go quickly!"

Dan turned at last and opened the door. Madame de la Fontaine called sharply to the waiting Jean, and he, motioning to Dan to follow him, led the way on deck. In a moment they were in a little boat heading for the shore. The afternoon sun was bright in the western sky. *The Southern Cross* rode serenely at anchor, and from her deck, Madame de la Fontaine was waving him good-bye.

CHAPTER XVII

THE MARQUIS LEAVES THE INN

By the time Dan was put ashore on the beach of the Cove it was afternoon. During the short row from the schooner he had been unable to exchange remarks with the surly Jean, for that individual's only response to his repeated efforts, was a surly *"Je ne parle pas anglais,"* which seemed to answer as a general formula to the conspirators. He gave up at last in disgust, and waited impatiently for the small boat to be beached, distrustful lest at the last moment some fresh trick be played upon him. Not that his ingenuous faith in the beautiful French lady failed him, but he was suspicious lest, having acted independently of the Marquis and Captain Bonhomme in releasing him, she should not have the power to make that release genuinely effective.

But his apprehensions were groundless. The seaman rowed straight for the shore, beached the boat with a last sturdy pull at the oars, and leaping out into the curling surf, held the skiff steady.

222

"Thank you very much," said Dan, shaking the spray from his coat.

"Eh?" grunted Jean.

"Oh!—beg pardon!—*merci*," he explained, exaggerating the pronunciation of the French word.

"Huh!" was the gutteral reply, as the man jumped back into the skiff, and pushed off. Dan looked once more towards the distant schooner and the slight figure in the stern. Then he started at a rapid pace for the Inn.

As he turned into the avenue of maples, he was surprised to see Jesse standing on the gallery, musket in hand, as though he were a sentinel on guard.

"Bless my soul, Mister Dan! I thought the Frenchies had made way with you. You're a blessed sight to lay eyes on. But Mister Tom was right, he said you'd be coming back this afternoon."

"Well, here I am, Jesse," Dan replied grasping his hand, "as large as life and twice as natural, I guess. I feel as if I'd been away for a year and a day. But tell me, what's the news? Where is Tom? Has Nancy come back? How is Mother? Have you been having trouble, that you are guarding the door like a soldier on duty?"

"Well, now, Mister Dan, one at a time, *if* you please. Can't say exactly as we've been havin' trouble; but we've sort of been lookin' for it. And Mister Tom—"

"Where is Tom? I must see him at once.'

"He ain't here, sir; he left about an hour ago, driving the old Miss and Miss Nancy to the Red Farm, sir; so as to be out of harm's way. He'll be back before night, sir."

"Ah, good! Then Nance is back? When did she come?"

"She come back last night, sir; leastways Mister Tom brought her back. Mister Tom, he got the idea that they'd cooped Miss Nance up on that there schooner laying in the Cove, and sure enough, he found her there and got her off somehows last night."

"Good for Tom! How did he work it?"

"I ain't heard no particulars, Mister Dan. We've been too busy watching things to talk much. We got Ezra Manners out from the Port to help do guard duty."

"Guard?—what?"

"Why, the Inn, sir. Mister Tom he's been sort of expectin' some kind of attack. That's the reason he took the women folks over to the Red Farm."

"I see—and where's the old Marquis?"

Jesse chuckled. "The old Marquis's where he hasn't been doin' any harm for the last twenty-four hours, sir. Mister Tom he locked him up last night in one of the south bedrooms. That reminds me, I was to let him out just as soon as you come back."

"Why lock him up, and then let him out? Things have been moving at the Inn, Jess, since I've been gone!"

"Moving—yes, sir. But them's my orders—first thing I was to do soon as you come back was to let the old Frenchy out and do as he pleased. Mister Tom was to arrange everything else with you, sir."

"Seems as if Tom had a whole campaign planned out. All right—we'll obey orders, Jess. Let the Marquis out, and tell him he can find me in the bar if he wants to see me. What time will Tom be back?"

"Before dark, sir, I'm sure. He's been gone over an hour."

Dan ran up to his bedroom, made a quick toilet, took the torn scrap of paper from his strong-box, and put it in his wallet. Then he went down stairs into the bar. The Marquis, released from his confinement, was awaiting him.

"Ah, Monsieur Frost!" the old gentleman exclaimed, coming forward with outstretched hands, "I rejoice at your return. Now this so horrible nightmare will end.... Ah!" This last exclamation was uttered in a tone of surprise and indignation, for Dan faced him with folded arms, deliberately refusing the handclasp.

"Yes, Marquis," he said, "I have returned; but I cannot say that I am particularly pleased to see you."

"Monsieur, *te me comprends pas;* this abuse, this insult—it is impossible that I understand."

"Pray, Monsieur de Boisdhyver," replied Dan, with dignity, "Let us have done with make-believe and sham. For two days I have been in prison on that confounded ship yonder, whose villainous crew are in your pay."

"You in prison—the ship—the villainous crew!" repeated the Marquis. "What is it that you say?"

"Come, Marquis, your protests are useless," Dan interrupted. "I know of the conspiracy in which you are engaged, of your deceit and trickery here,

of your part in my poor sister's disappearance.
You know that Madame de la Fontaine has told
me much. Do you expect me to meet you as
though nothing had happened?"

"But, *mon cher, monsieur*," continued the Marquis, "if it is that you have been told anything
by Madame de la Fontaine, my so good friend,
the bright angel of an old age too-cruelly shattered
by misfortune, you well know how innocent are
my designs, how sincere my efforts for your foster-
sister, for her who is my niece."

"Marquis, I do not understand all that has
taken place. I may say further that I do not care
to discuss the situation with you until I have
talked with my sister and Mr. Pembroke."

"Ah! then Eloise—then Mademoiselle Nancy,
is returned?" exclaimed the old gentleman.

"I believe so. But I have not seen her. I must
decline, Marquis, to continue this conversation.
I must first learn what has taken place in my absence. When Tom returns—he is out just now—
I am perfectly willing to talk matters over with
you and him together."

The Marquis's eyes flashed. "But, Monsieur,"
he protested, "you must understand that I cannot submit to meet with Monsieur Pembroke

again. A Marquis de Boisdhyver does not twice put himself in the position to be insulted with impunity."

"I should hardly imagine," Dan replied, "that it would be more difficult for you to meet Pembroke again than it has been difficult for me to meet you."

"How—me?—*je ne comprends pas*. But I have been insulted, imprisoned, I have suffered much that is terrible."

"I found myself in an identical situation," said Dan.

"But, monsieur, *un moment*," protested the old gentleman, as Dan made as if to leave the room, "give me the time to explain to you this misunderstanding.—"

"No, Marquis. I will not talk until I have seen Tom."

The black eyes of Monsieur de Boisdhyver gleamed unpleasantly. "I have said to you, Monsieur Frost, that I refuse to meet Monsieur Tom Pembroke once more. It would be intolerable. *Impossible, absolutment!* I must insist that you will be kind enough to facilitate my departure at once."

"Certainly, as you wish, Marquis."

The old gentleman hesitated. For once inde-
cision was shown by the agitation of his features
and the shifting of his eyes, but he gave no other
expression to the quandaries in his mind. After
a moment's silence he drew himself up with ex-
aggerated dignity. With one hand upon his breast
and the other extended, in a fashion at once absurd and a little pathetic, he addressed Dan for
the last time, as might an ambassador taking leave
of a sovereign upon his declaration of war.

"Monsieur, I renew my gratitude for the hospitality of the Inn at the Red Oak, so long enjoyed, so discourteously withdrawn. I require but
the presentation of my account for the time, I
have trespassed upon your good will, and I request the assistance of a servant to facilitate my
departure. But I do not take my farewell without protesting, *ovec tout mon coeur,* at the misunderstanding to which I am persistently subjected. The inevitable bitterness in my soul does
not prevent me even now to forget the sweet hours
of rest that I have enjoyed here. The unwilling-
ness on your part, monsieur, to comprehend my
position, does not interfere to stifle in my breast
the consciousness but of honourable purpose. I
make my compliments to mesdames."

"Very good, marquis—and at what time shall I have a carriage ready for you?"

The Marquis glanced nonchalantly at his watch, "In fifteen minutes, monsieur."

"It will be ready, Marquis."

"Your very obedient servant; Monsieur Frost."

"Your obedient servant, Marquis de Boisdhyver."

The old gentleman bowed again with elaborate courtesy and, turning sharply on his heel, left the room.

Somewhat disturbed by the turn affairs had taken, Dan stood for a moment lost in thought. There was nothing for it, he supposed: Tom, who had been in command, had given orders, and they should be obeyed; besides there was no reason that he could see why the Marquis should be detained at the Inn of he chose to leave it. So he sat down at a table, made out the old gentleman's bill for the month, and then stepped to the door to call for Jesse.

"Take this," he said when the man appeared in response to his summons, "to the old Marquis. It is the bill for his board. If he pays you, well and good; if not—in any case, treat him courteously, and do not interfere with his movements. He is leaving the Inn for good. I want you to have the buggy ready within half-an-hour and drive him where he wishes to go. I fancy he will want his stuff put on the schooner in the Cove."

"All right, sir," replied Jesse. "Now that you and Miss Nance are back, sir, I guess the sooner we get rid of the Marquis the better."

Jesse carried the bill to the Marquis, then came down and went to the barn to harness the horse. A little later he drove round to the courtyard, hitched the horse to a ring in the Red Oak, and ran upstairs to fetch the Marquis's boxes.

Perhaps half-an-hour had passed when he returned to Dan in the Bar. "The old gentleman's gone, sir," he said.

"Gone!—where?" cried Dan.

"Don't know, sir," Jesse replied. "To the schooner, I guess. He left this money on his dressing-bureau."

Dan took the gold which Jesse held out to him. "Well, well," he murmured, "quite on his dignity, eh? All right, Jess, take his stuff to the beach and hail the schooner. He will probably have given directions. I hope we've seen the last of him."

PART IV
THE ATTACK ON THE INN.

CHAPTER XVIII

THE AVENUE OF MAPLES

The Marquis's belongings were sent after him to the schooner, where, however, it appeared that they had not been expected, for it was some time before Jesse could obtain an answer to his hail from the shore, and still longer before he could make the men on the ship understand what it was he wanted with them. Eventually Captain Bonhomme had rowed ashore, and the Marquis's bags, boxes, writing-desk, and fiddle were loaded into the small boat and taken off to *The Southern Cross.*

It appeared from Jesse's report that the Captain had been sufficiently polite, and had attributed the misunderstanding of his men to their inability to speak English. They had not gotten

their orders for the Marquis.   He had asked no
further questions about Monsieur de Boisdhyver
or about his recent prisoners, but had feed Jesse
liberally, and dismissed him, with his own and the
Marquis's thanks.

"Well," said Tom, who had returned an hour before and had been exchanging experiences with
Dan, "that seems to be the end of him for the
present.   I don't know that I did right in promising your French lady that I should release him,
but there seemed no other way to make sure of
getting you back."

"I am glad you promised," replied Dan.   "It is
a relief not to have him under our roof.   For the
last week I've felt as if the place were haunted by
an evil spirit."

"So it has been, and so it still will be, I am
afraid," was Tom's reply.   "If there is treasure
here, you may be sure that gang won't sail away
without making a desperate effort to get it.   I
move that we beat them out by hunting for it ourselves.   Why not begin to-night?"

"Not to-night," protested Dan.   "I am tired to
death.   You can imagine that I didn't get much
sleep cooped up on that confounded ship."

"No more have I, old boy.   But I believe in

striking while the iron is hot. Every day's delay gives them a better chance for their plans, if they mean to attack the Inn."

"I doubt if they'll do that. I don't think force is precisely their line. You know, I believe that the story Madame de la Fontaine told isn't altogether a fiction."

"Pshaw!" exclaimed Tom. "I don't believe a word of it. Naturally they wouldn't use force, if they could help it. But their plans have all been upset, and a gang like that won't stop at anything."

"But we live in a civilized community, my boy. This isn't the middle ages."

"We live in a civilized community, perhaps; but if you can find a more isolated spot, a place more remote from help, in any other part of the civilized world, I'd be glad to see it. We might as well be in the middle of the Sahara desert. Find the treasure and get it out of harm's way—that's my idea."

"All right, but to-morrow; I swear I'm not up to it to-night."

"To-morrow! Well, then to-morrow. Though for the life of me, I don't see why you want to delay things. Jesse and Ezra can keep watch to-night."

"But we must get some sleep, Tom."

"The devil with sleep! However, you're the boss now. It's your inn, your treasure, your sister, that are involved. I'll take a back seat."

"Come, come, Tom—don't let's quarrel. Give me to-night to—to get myself together, and to-morrow I'll pull the Inn down with you, if you wish."

Perhaps Dan was right, he did need rest and sleep and a few hours would restore him. They had their supper, then, apportioned the night into watches, and Dan went upstairs for his first period of sleep.

His brain was a-whirl. All through the afternoon, during his talk with the Marquis, and later during his talk with Tom, one idea had been dominating his thought, dictating his plan of action, colouring his judgment. The fascination which Madame de la Fontaine exerted over his senses was too strong for him even to contemplate resisting it. She was confessedly in league with a gang of adventurers upon a quest for treasure. She had lied to him at first about the Marquis, she had lied to him about Nancy, she had lied to him about his release; and when she had left him under the pretext of arranging his return to the Inn, she had in fact gone to Tom to bargain an exchange of him for the old Marquis. Her lies, her subterfuges, her flatteries, had been evidently designed but to get possession of the torn scrap of paper which was so necessary to their finding the hidden treasure. All this Dan told himself a hundred times, and then, quickly dispelling the witness of these cold hard facts, there would flash before him the vision of her wonderful eyes, of her strange appealing beauty, of her stirring personality; he would feel once more the touch of her cheek and her lips pressing his, intoxicating as wine; and delicious fires flamed through his veins, and set his heart to beating, and made havoc of his honour and his conscience. Whatever were the consequences, he would meet her again that night as he had promised. It was his first experience of passion and it was sweeping him off his feet.

Alone in his room Dan sat down at the table. He drew from his pocket the torn paper, and as an act of justice to the friends he felt that he was about to betray, he labourously made a copy of the difficult French handwriting. This done, he locked the copy in his strong box and put the original back in his pocket. Then, like the criminal he thought himself to be, he crept cautiously down the stairs. The door into the bar was open, and he stood for a moment, shoes in hand, peering into the dimly-lit room. Tom sat by the hearth, reading, a pipe in his mouth and a cocked pistol on the table by his side. A pang went through Dan's breast, but he checked the impulse to speak, and stole softly across the hall and into his mother's parlour. Ever so cautiously he closed the door behind him, crossed the room, and raised the sash of one of the windows.

It was dark, but starlight; the moon had not yet risen. In a moment he had slipped over the sill and stood upon the porch. Lowering the sash, he crept across the band of light that shone from the windows of the bar, and into the shadow of the Red Oak. There he buttoned his great coat tightly about him, put on his shoes, and started softly down the avenue of maples. Scarcely a sound disturbed the silence of the night, save the lazy creaking of the windmill as it turned now and then to the puff of a gentle breeze.

At every few steps, he paused to listen, fearful lest his absence had been detected and he were followed by some one from the Inn. Then he would start on again, peering eagerly into the darkness ahead for any sign of her whom he sought. At last he reached the end of the avenue. His heart was beating wildly, in a very terror that she might not come. Nothing—no catastrophe, no danger, no disgrace,—could be so terrible to him as that the woman he loved so recklessly and madly should not come. She must not fail! He looked at his watch; it was already three minutes past ten. If in five—then minutes she did not come, he would go to seek her—to the House on the Dunes, aye, if must be to *The Southern Cross* itself.

Suddenly a dark figure slipped out of the gloom, and Claire de la Fontaine was in his arms. For a moment she let him clasp her, let his lips again meet hers; then quickly she disengaged herself. "Are we safe?" she asked in a whisper. "Is it that we can talk here."

"We are perfectly safe," he answered. "Nothing can be heard from the Inn. No one is about."

"You escaped without notice? Are you certain that no one follows you?"

"Absolutely. I am sure. And you?"

"I?—Oh, no, no—. There is no one to question me. I have been at the House on the Dunes all the evening. Marie, my maid,—she thinks that I am gone to the schooner. *Mon Dieu! cher ami,* what terrors I have suffered for you. It had not seemed possible that Claire de la Fontaine would ride and walk two so long miles in a desolate country to meet a lover—It must be that we are gone mad."

"Madness then is the sweetest experience of life," said Dan, seizing her hand again and carrying it to his lips.

"Ah *peut-être, mon ami.* But now there are many affairs to discuss. Tell me—the Marquis, he was released, as your friend has promised me he should be?"

"Of course, didn't you know it?"

"I know nothing. Why then is it he has not left the Inn?"

"But he did leave—in the middle of the afternoon, half an hour after I returned."

"And where is it that he has gone?"

"To the schooner, I suppose. He left alone, giving directions for his things to be sent after him."

"Ah! to the schooner, you say? You are certain?"

"Yes—that is, I think he went there. Jesse took his boxes and bags down to the shore, and

Captain Bonhomme received them, and thanked him in the Marquis's name."

"Mais non! Est-ce possible?" For a moment she was silent, considering deeply. *"Bien!"* she exclaimed presently. "It is as you say, of course. And you, my friend?" She stopped suddenly, for they had been walking slowly forward, and withdrawing her hand from his arm, she held it out before him. "The paper?" she demanded.

"Here it is," murmured Dan, fumbling in his pocket, and pulling out the scrap of paper. She took it eagerly from his hand and held it up before her eyes as though trying to see it in the dark.

"This is it, really?" she asked.

"I swear it," he answered. "It is the piece of writing that I found in the hidden cubbyhole of the old cabinet in the Oak Parlour. It is written in French, you know."

"Yes, I know, I know," she assented absently. For a moment she was quite still, and then, with a strange exclamation, she put the paper to her lips. *"Quels souvenirs d'autrefois!"* she murmured. *"Ah, mon Dieu, mon Dieu!"*

"Dearest, what is it?" asked Dan.

"Nothing, nothing," she replied, "withdrawing a little from his touch. "I was unwell for the moment,—*ce ne fait rien.* No, no, you are not to kiss me, please." Again she unloosed his arm from about her neck, slipped the paper into her muff, and pressed a little forward. For a space they walked slowly, silently, toward the Inn.

"But, dearest one," murmured Dan, "this proves to you my love, doesn't it? You no longer doubt me. For your sake, I give my honour; it may be, the safety of my friends. You must see how I love you with all my heart and soul. Won't you,—"

Suddenly she stopped again quite still and faced him. "My poor boy," she said gently, "you really love me?"

"Love you! My God, have I not proved it! What more would you have me do?"

"*Mais oui,*" she answered quickly. "You have proved it, but I have thought that it was not possible."

"And you—you do care—oh, tell me—"

"*Hélas, mon pauvre ami.* I love as tenderly as it remains in me to love. Ah, dear, dear boy, so sincerely, that I cannot have you to sell your honour for the futile kisses of Claire de la Fontaine."

"What do you mean? Have I—"

"No, no, no! This—take the paper. You must not again give it me, I desire that you will not." She drew the paper from her muff with an impulsive movement and thrust it toward him. "Take it, I implore you."

"But why—?"

"Because that you shall not give your honour to a woman such as I am. *Mai vraiment,* I love you. That is why you must take back the paper."

"But you must explain—"

"*Mon Dieu!* is it that I have not explained? There is time for nothing more. I have fear, *mon ami;* a kiss, and it is necessary that I go. It is good-bye."

"But you love me, you have said so. I cannot, I will not let you go."

"Listen to me, my friend," she said, her voice rising for the moment above the whisper in which she had cautiously spoken heretofore. "From the first I have deceived you, betrayed you, played upon your affection but to betray you afresh. And now I find that I love you. I am not that which you call good, but it is impossible that I injure you. Go back to your friends."

"Never! I love you. What matters now anything that you have said or done? And you love me. Ah dearest one, what can that mean but good?"

"*Bien-aimé,* what will you that I say?" she interrupted speaking rapidly, "I am what you Americans call 'a bad woman',—the sort of woman that you know nothing of. I was the woman who sixteen years ago stayed at the Inn at the Red Oak with François de Boisdhyver, the woman your mother called nurse, who cared for his little daughter. And now I have told you all. Will you know from now that I am a thousand times unworthy? *Pour l'amour de Dieu,* give it to me to do this one act of honour and of generosity."

CHAPTER XIX

THE ATTACK

With these words she thrust the scrap of paper into his hands and turning swiftly, started forward as though to escape his further importunities by flight. But Dan was instantly by her side, trying to catch her hand in the darkness.

Again she faced him passionately. *"C'est folie,"* she cried hoarsely, "have I not told you that we are in great danger? Go, go back to the Inn. It is there only that you will be safe.—*O, mon Dieu!"*

A figure had sprung suddenly from the blackness of the trees. Dan felt a sharp blow on his shoulder, and then he was grappling with a wiry antagonist, striving to keep at safe distance a hand that clutched an open knife. Locked in a close embrace, swaying from side to side of the road, they fought desperately. Dan striving to get at the pistol which he carried, his assailant trying to use his knife.

It seemed as if Dan could no longer hold the

244

man off when two small hands closed over the fist
that held the gleaming knife and a clear voice rang
out in French. Dan felt his antagonist's grip
loosen and he wrenched himself free. Madame de
la Fontaine had come to his rescue. "Quick, quick
—to the Inn. I am safe. You have but one
chance for your life," she cried. Already his assailant had put a boatswain's whistle to his lips
and was sounding a shrill blast.

As Dan hesitated, uncertain what to do, he
heard a number of men come crashing through the
underbrush of the neighbouring field. Again Madame de la Fontaine cried, *"Mon Dieu!* will you
not run?" Then she turned and disappeared in
the darkness. Simultaneously came the crack of
a pistol shot, and a bullet whizzed by his ear.
There was nothing for it but to run; and run he
did, shouting at the top of his voice the while to
Tom in the Inn. He probably owed his start to
the fact that for the moment his attacker, who had
been held at bay by Madame de la Fontaine, was
uncertain whether to follow her or Dan. That
moment's delay saved Dan's life, for though, with
a curse, the man started after him now, he had
a poor chance of catching him in the darkness.
But on he came only a dozen yards or so behind,

and after him the thundering steps and harsh cries of those who had responded to the call of the whistle.

At last Dan was at the door of the Inn, beating wildly upon it, and calling, "Open, Tom; quick, for God's sake! It's Dan." As the door was flung back, he sprang in and slammed it shut. Already the attackers were in the courtyard, a volley of shots rang against the stout oak, followed almost at once, by the flinging against it of half-a-dozen men. But the great oaken beam had been slipped into place and held firmly. Dan was none the worse for his experience, save for a graze on the cheek where the knife had glanced, and a slit on his shoulder from a bullet.

"They're here!" he cried. "No time for explanations, Tom. I went out—fool that I was!—was attacked. They're here in force."

By this time Jesse had rushed into the bar, attracted by the firing, and soon Ezra Manners came running down from the floor above. After the first impact against the door those without had withdrawn, evidently taking up a position in the courtyard again, for almost at once there was a fusilade of shots against door and windows, which luckily the heavy oak was proof against.

"They're welcome to keep that up all night," said Tom. "Only a waste of ammunition. How many are there?" He would liked to have asked Dan why he had gone out, but there was no time for discussion.

"I don't know—half-a-dozen at least, I should guess," was Dan's reply. "Bonhomme is at their head, I'm sure. It was he who tackled me in the avenue. They may have the whole crew of the schooner here. That would mean a dozen or more."

"Well," said Tom, "we're in for it now, I guess. We'll have to watch in different parts of the house, for we don't know where they will attack. Unless they are all fools, it won't be here."

"You're right. I'll stay and look out for the south wing. You go to the north wing, Tom; Jesse to the kitchen, and Ezra to the end of the south passage. That 'll cover the house as well as we can cover it. They'll try to force an entrance somewheres. Have you all got guns? Good. Leave the doors open so that we can hear each other call."

Evidently the attacking party had concluded that they were wasting their lead and their time in shooting at doors and window-shutters, for as

Tom had said, all was now quiet outside. Fifteen minutes, half-an-hour passed, and nothing occurred to alarm or to relieve the tension on the anxious watchers within. At length Dan stole upstairs to reconnoitre.

It was fortunate that he chose the precise moment he did, for as his head emerged above the last stair, he saw that the great shutters at the end of the south corridor were open, and a man stood before the window, evidently on the top rung of a ladder, trying the sash. It was locked to be sure, but at the instant Dan saw him, he raised his fist and smashed it. He was about to leap through the opening, fringed though it was with jagged glass, when Dan aimed his pistol carefully, and fired. There was a cry, and the form at the window fell crashing to the ground below. Dan rushed to the casement, and could hear in the court beneath him the curses and exclamations of the surprised assailants. Quickly he thrust the end of the ladder from the wall, then seizing a fresh pistol from his belt, fired at random into the darkness below. Another cry of pain attested to the fact that his chance shot had taken effect. By this time Tom had rushed to his assistance, and together they barred the window again.

Dan gave a brief account of the incident. "But, for heaven's sake, Tom," he concluded, "get back to the north wing. We are in danger there every moment. I'll watch out here."

As Tom returned to his post in the cold corridor of the north wing, he heard heavy crashes, as of a battering-ram, against the great door that opened into the gallery. A shrill whistle brought Ezra Manners to his assistance. "Watch here!" he commanded. "If the door crashes in, shoot, and shoot to kill; then run into the bar and barricade the door between. I've a plan."

He himself ran into the bar, blew out the candles, and risking perhaps too much on the chance of success, cautiously opened the front door. He could scarcely make out the group at the farther end of the gallery, as he stepped out; but he could hear the resounding crashes against the door into the north hall, each one of which seemed to be the last that even that massive frame could hold out against. Leveling his pistol at the group; he took aim, and fired; snatched another from his pocket, and fired a second time. Again, by good luck, the defender's shots had told. There was a thud on the gallery floor, and the besiegers scurried to cover beyond the courtyard fence. Tom dashed safely back into the house, and slipped the great beam into place.

Upstairs Dan's attention had been attracted by the commotion in front of the inn. He opened a window on to the roof of the gallery, climbed out, and crawled along on his belly till his head just abutted over the eaves. For a few moments, after the firing, he could hear the attackers moving about behind the fence across the courtyard. At length, a couple of them stole across the court and up on to the gallery beneath him. In a moment they returned carrying the dead or wounded comrade; then all of them seemed to go off together up the dark avenue of maples. He waited till they could be heard no more, then crept back into the house and ran down to tell Dan of their temporary withdrawal. For an hour or more the four defenders of the Inn kept themselves occupied parading the corridors and rooms, on the watch for a fresh attack. But nothing happened. They felt no security, however, and would feel none till daylight.

In the silent watching of that night Dan had ample opportunity to reflect upon his extraordinary interview with Madame de la Fontaine. He loved her. Good heavens how he loved her, but—

had she been sincere in her refusal at the last to keep the scrap of paper for the possession of which she had so desperately intrigued? Had she decoyed him to the rendezvous in the dark but to betray him to the bandits with whom she was in league? At first it would seem so. And yet the paper was in his possession; and, she it was who had rescued him from the assassin's knife. Where was she now? What had become of her? What was to be the end of this mad night's work? That she was the woman who had accompanied General Pointelle—or the Maréchal de Boisdhyver—somehow did not surprise him. And for the time the full import of what that implied did not dawn upon him. But what mattered anything now that he loved her?

He determined at last to reconnoitre again from the roof of the gallery. It still lay in shadow, but it would not be long before the moon, now rising over the eastern hills beyond the Strathsey flooded it with light. In a moment, he had opened the window, was over the sill, and, creeping cautiously along the roof to the ledge, he worked his way toward the great oak at the farther end.

All was still and deserted below as the Inn courtyard would have been in the middle of any

winter's night. While he stood peering into the
darkness, listening intently, the moon, just showing above the distant tree tops, cast the first rays
of its light into the courtyard beneath him. At
the instant the figure of a woman stole across the
flagged pavement and crept fearfully to the Red
Oak. With a strange thrill he recognized Claire
de la Fontaine. Reaching the shelter of the great
tree, she stooped, gathered a handful of gravel
from the road bed, and then cast it boldly at the
shutters of the bar, calling softly, "Dan, Dan."

Instantly he replied. "Claire! Is that you?
What is it? I am here, above you, on the roof."

"Ah, *mon Dieu!*" she exclaimed, as she looked
up startled, and discerned his form leaning over
the eaves, "for the love of heaven, my friend, open
to me. I am in danger and I must tell you that
which is of great importance to you. *Mais vite,
mon ami.* In ten minutes they will return
again."

It did not occur to Dan to doubt her. Careless
of the risk, he rushed back to the window, climbed
in, and in a few seconds had opened the door to
the anxious woman without. She seemed physi-
cally exhausted as she stepped into the warm bar.
Taking her in his arms, he carried her to a chair,

and poured out a glass of wine, which she eagerly drank.

"It matters not what I have been doing," she murmured in reply to his questions, "I have but little time to give you my warning. *Ecoute*. Bonhomme and his men are gone only to carry back their dead and wounded, and to bring cutlasses, and the two or three sailors who were left on the schooner. I have followed them—God knows how —and heard something of their plans. They will make an attack—now, in a moment—in two different places. But these attacks will be shams,— is not that the word?—they will mean nothing. It is the Oak Parlour that they desire to enter. At the window of that so horrible room Bonhomme will try to make an entrance without alarm while the others hold your attention at the front and back of the Inn. Is it that you understand? It is necessary that you are prepared for these sham attacks, but the great danger is Bonhomme. The window in the Oak Parlour is not strong. They have information—recent information— from the Marquis probably,—that it will not be difficult to break in. One of you must conceal himself in the dark and shoot Bonhomme when he enters; you must shoot and shoot to kill, then we will be safe. I have no fear of Monsieur le Marquis. The others—they are brutes—but they will flee. And they know nothing, they do this for money,—ah, *mon Dieu*, for money which I have furnished!"

For a moment, torn between his love and his deep distrust of this woman, poor Dan stood uncertainly. Suddenly he knelt at her side and clasped his arms about her. "Claire, you are on our side? You swear it."

"Ah, *mon Dieu!* is it that I deserve this?" she exclaimed bitterly. "Ah! I tell you truth," she cried. "You must believe me—Listen! Are they come already?"

"No, no, there is nothing. But I trust you, I will go."

Suddenly she sprang to her feet. "Let me go with you. It is terrible to me to enter again that room; but I desire to prove myself of honour. *Allons, allons!*"

"Tom is there."

"Ah! send him here to the bar. But do you come, *mon ami.* See, I go with you." She rose and forcing herself to the effort, led the way across the bar and into the corridor of the north wing, as if to show him that in sixteen years she had not forgotten.

CHAPTER XX

"You know the way?" Dan exclaimed as he caught up with her, and held open the door that led into the old north wing.

"But so well," she replied, catching her breath. "Would to God that I did not!"

"Ah!" he murmured, "I forgot that you have been here before."

They pressed on silently. At the turn of the corridor upon which the Oak Parlour gave, they discerned Tom Pembroke, a weird figure, in the dim light of the tallow dip upon the table, that cast fantastic shadows upon the whitewashed walls.

As he recognized them, he sprang forward in astonishment. "Madame de la Fontaine! Dan! What does this mean?" he cried.

"You know Madame?" Dan replied hastily and in evident confusion. "At great risk she has come to warn us—she is our friend, understand.—She has come to tell us how Bonhomme and his men will attack the Inn."

Tom listened to his explanation with unconcealed dismay. "Good heavens, Dan!" he protested, "You trust this woman? You know she is in league with these ruffians. Do you want us to fall into a trap?"

"No, no, Monsieur Pembroke," interrupted Madame de la Fontaine, "you must listen to me. I understand your fear. But at last you can trust me. I repent that which I have done. Ah, *mon Dieu,* with what bitterness! And now I desire to do all that is possible to save you. You must trust me."

"I do not—I can not trust you," Tom cried sternly. "Don't go in there, Dan. Don't I beg of you, trust this woman's word. It is a trick."

"Perhaps," said Dan grimly, "but go back. I take the responsibility. I do trust her, I shall trust her—to death. There is no time to lose, man. Go back!"

"What deviltry has bewitched you?" cried Tom passionately. "Already once to-night you have risked our lives by your fool-hardiness,—for the sake of this woman, eh? By gad, man, I begin to see. But I tell you now, I refuse to be a victim to your madness."

"*Mais non*, Monsieur Pembroke," Claire cried again. "By all that is good and holy, I swear to you, that that which I have said is true. You must go. They will attack the bar and the kitchen. If those places are not defended, there will be danger."

"At any rate," said Dan," I am going into the Oak Parlour. If you refuse to act with me, barricade the door between the bar and the north wing. If need be, I shall fight alone. Only now we lose time, precious time."

Pembroke looked at him as if he had gone mad, then shrugging his shoulders he turned back into the bar, whistling for Jesse and Ezra as he did so.

For a moment, glancing after Tom's retreating figure, shaken to his soul by conflicting emotions, Dan stood irresolute.

"But come," said Madame de la Fontaine, touching his arm. Again like the weird genius of this strange night she led the way on down the shadowy hall, and paused only when her hand rested upon the knob of the door into the Oak Parlour. "It is here," she said simply.

As Dan reached her side, she opened the door.
The light of the candle down the hallway did not
penetrate the gloom of the disused room.   A
musty smell as of cold stagnant air came strong to
their nostrils, and Dan felt, as they crossed the
threshold together, that he was entering a place
where no life had been for a long long time, a place
full of dead nameless horrors.

The woman by his side was trembling violently.
He put his arm about her to reassure her, and
there shot through him a sensation of strange and
terrible joy to be with her alone in this darkness
and danger.   For the moment he was exulting that
for her sake he had risked his honour, that for her
sake now he was risking life itself.   He bent his
head to hers.

"No! no!—not here!" she whispered hoarsely,
but yet clinging to him with shaking hands.   "It
is so cold, so dark.   I have fear," she murmured.

"It is like a tomb," he said.

"The tomb of my hopes, of my youth," she
breathed softly.

"Shall I strike a light?"

"No, no,—no light, I implore you.   *Ecoute!*
What is it that I hear?"

"I hear nothing.   It is the wind in the Red Oak outside."

"But listen!"

"It is an owl hooting."

Suddenly she drew her hand from his, and he could hear her moving swiftly about. "All is as it used to be?" she asked.

"Precisely," he answered; "nothing has been changed."

"Here is the cabinet," she said, from across the room. "I can feel the lion's head. It is opposite to the window and the moonlight will stream in when the casement is opened, but if I crouch low I shall not be seen. *Bien!* And you, *mon ami?* Tell me, is the old *escritoire* still to the left of the door?" Now she was back at his side once again.

"The *escritoire?*" he repeated.

"The little table where one writes. Ah! yes, it is here. See, behind this, *mon ami,* shall you hide yourself. The moonlight will not reach here—and it is so arranged that you will see plainly any one that appears at the window. When the casement is opened, you will shoot, will you not, and shoot to kill?"

"Yes, I will shoot," said Dan, his voice trembling.

"You promise me?" she cried in a tense whisper, as she grasped his arm and held it tight in her grip.

"I tell you, yes."

"You must not fail."

"No. Shall I shoot at any one who opens?"

"Any one?—it will be Bonhomme,—no other."

Suddenly there came, from the front and the rear of the Inn, at the same instant it seemed, the sharp staccato of a fusilade of pistol shots, and the lumbering blows as of beams being thrust at distant doors.

"They are come!" she whispered, "hide." Dan could hear the swish of her garments as she rapidly glided across the room to the old cabinet, then he turned and crouched low behind the writing desk that she had chosen for his place of concealment. He knelt there motionless, a cocked pistol clenched in his right hand. His breath seemed to have stopped, but his heart was pounding as though it must burst through his breast. How could he shoot down in cold blood a fellow man? The horror of it crowded out all other impressions, sensations fears. He could fight, risk his life, but to pull the trigger of that pistol when the casement should open seemed to him an impossibility. He would wait, grapple with him, fight as men should.

Suddenly a ray of moonlight fell across the dark floor. Dan, looking up, seemed frozen by horror. The shutters had opened, the casement swung back noiselessly, and there in the opening, sharply outlined against the moonlight-flooded night, was the great black hulk of Captain Bonhomme.

For a moment he stood there irresolute, listening intently. Dan was fascinated, motionless, held as in a vice by the horror of the thing.

Suddenly Bonhomme moved his head to one side as if to listen more acutely. As he did so, the ray of moonlight fell upon the cabinet, fell upon Claire de la Fontaine, upon something that she held in an outstretched hand that gleamed.

"Nom de Dieu!" There was the flash and crack of a pistol, a sharp cry, and the great figure fell back and sank out of sight.

With that Dan sprang forward, reckless of danger, and ran to the window. He heard without the confused sounds as of persons scurrying to cover, saw their forms dash across the moonlit courtyard, into the shadows of the trees and outhouses. Beneath him on the floor of the gallery was something horrible and still.

Almost instantly Claire de la Fontaine was by

his side, and as regardless of danger as he, she was calling sharply, calling men by their names. Her hair had been loosened and fell over her shoulders in black waves, her dark eyes flashed with excitement and passion, and her face, strangely pale, in the silver moonlight, was set in stern harsh lines. Even then this vision of her tragic beauty thrilled the man at her side.

But she was as unconscious of him as she was of her danger. With hand uplifted she called by name the desperados, who had taken shelter in the darkness and to those who now came running from front and rear where their attacks had been unsuccessful.

Appalled, spell-bound by the vision, even as Dan was, they stopped, and stood listening mutely to the torrent of words that she poured forth,— vehement French of which Dan had no understanding.

At last, ending the frightful tension of the scene, two of the men came forward, crept up to the lifeless body of Bonhomme, and grasping it by head and feet, carried it away, across the courtyard, into the darkness of the avenue of maples. One by one, still mysteriously silent, the others of the gang followed, till at length the last one had disappeared into the gloom. Weird silence fell once more upon the Inn.

It was only then that Madame de la Fontaine turned to Dan. "They will come no more," she said in a strained unnatural voice. "We are saved, safe.... I have proved, is it not so?—my honour, my love."

With the words she sank at his feet, just as Tom, candle in hand, appeared in the doorway.

CHAPTER XXI

THE TREASURE

Owing doubtless to the death of Bonhomme and to the orders given in no uncertain tones by Madame de la Fontaine, the bandits from the schooner in the cove did not make a further effort to attack the Inn that night. There was no rest, however, for Madame de la Fontaine, after her heroic exploit in the Oak Parlour, had swooned completely away. They carried her to the couch in Mrs. Frost's parlour, and, awkwardly enough, did what could be done for her by men. It was over an hour before they succeeded in restoring her to consciousness, and when they did so, she awoke to delirium and fever. Distracted by anxiety and by their helplessness, at the first streak of dawn, Dan started for town to get a doctor, and Ezra Manners volunteered to go to the Red Farm and bring back Mrs. Frost, Nancy, and the maids.

About six o'clock in the morning the women folk returned to the Inn. But the briefest account of the attack was given them, though they were told in no uncertain terms of Madame de la Fontaine's heroic action in coming to warn them and of her courageous shot at the leader. Then Mrs. Frost and Nancy turned all their attention to the sick woman, caring for her as tenderly and devotedly as if she were their own. Half-an-hour later Dan returned from Monday Port with the family doctor, a grave silent old gentleman, in whose skill and discretion they trusted. After making an examination of his patient, he nodded his head encouragingly; gave a few directions to Mrs. Frost, and then left, promising to return later in the morning with medicines and supplies.

At last, utterly worn out, the four men threw themselves on their beds and slept from sheer exhaustion. The sun was high in the sky when they came down stairs again and found Nancy waiting for them, and a smoking breakfast ready on the table. After greeting them, she pointed to the window, across the fields, almost bare of snow now and gleaming in the morning sunlight, to the bright waters of the cove. "See!" she cried, "the schooner has disappeared."

They both looked. "By Jove, it has!" exclaimed Tom, rushing to the other side of the room, and peering out at the shipless sea. "Heigho! that's a relief. Pray God we've seen the last of her. The Marquis gone, the schooner gone,—we three together once more! Perhaps we shall begin to live again. Ah!" he added more softly, glancing with sudden sympathy at Dan's white drawn face, "I forgot the poor woman across the hall."

Dan turned aside to hide his emotion, for though a load of anxiety had been lifted from his heart by the vanishing of *The Southern Cross*, he was sick with fear for the issue of the illness that had stricken down the woman he loved,—the woman who had proved her love for him by so terrible and so tragic a deed.

As though aware that for the moment they were best left together alone, Nancy slipped away into the kitchen.

"You love her, Dan?" asked Tom simply.

"Yes, Tom, with all my heart and soul. I staked my honour, my life, on her sincerity. And how she has proved that we were right to trust her! It can't be—she mustn't die—I couldn't bear it!"

"She'll be all right, old fellow, don't worry; trust to your mother and Nance. It is only the shock of the terrible things she went through last night. Come on, we must take something to eat. Here is Nancy back again.'

There was no doubt of the fact, *The Southern Cross* had sailed away, vanished in the night as mysteriously as a week before she had appeared in the Strathsey and found moorings in the Cove. They did not count on the certainty of her not reappearing, however; and that night and for many nights thereafter the Inn was securely barricaded and a watch was kept, but neither then nor ever did *The Southern Cross* spread her sails in those waters again. She and her crew disappeared from their lives as completely as from the seas that stretched around the coast of Deal.

Tom at once was for making a search in the Oak Parlour for the hidden treasure, but for the time Dan had no heart for the undertaking. He urged delay at least until Madame de la Fontaine had recovered; and as for Nancy she would not hear of it.

"I can't bear to think of it,—of the trouble, the crime, the suffering of which it has been the cause. When our poor lady recovers, she will tell us all we need to know. I dread the Oak Parlour. I would not go into that room for anything in the world. Nor, believe me, Tom, could Dan do so now. You have guessed, haven't you, that he loves Madame de la Fontaine?"

"Of course, dearest; poor fellow! he betrays his love by every word and act. But good heaven, Nance, he couldn't marry her!"

"No—I don't know. I suppose not. But Dan will do as he will. To oppose him now would only make him the more wretched."

"Does your mother kow?"

"No, and it is best she should not. I don't think she has the faintest suspicion."

"Well, I suppose we had better let things rest awhile;" Tom assented, "but I swear I would like to get at the Oak Parlour and tear the secret out of it."

"We must wait a bit, Tom dear. Let's just be glad now of what we have and are."

And with that he drew her toward him and pressed for a definite answer to the question which so deeply concerned their future.

"When Madame has recovered, when we know all and the mystery is solved," she replied; then she added inconsequently, "I wonder if we shall ever hear of the old Marquis again."

"I wonder too," Tom exclaimed. "Though he has sailed away on *The Southern Cross*, I doubt if he will willingly leave the treasure behind him."

"That dreadful treasure, Tom," cried Nancy.

"I wish to goodness that the Marquis had it and might keep it always. We have each other."

The evening of the second day after the terrible night of the attack, as Dan was entering the Inn from his work outside, he saw Madame de la Fontaine standing on the gallery under the Red Oak. It was the dusk of a mild pleasant day. She was clad still in her soft grey gown with furs about her waists and neck, and a grey scarf over her head. But there was something infinitely pathetic to him in the listlessness of her attitude, in the expression of a deep and melancholy that had come into her face.

He stole swiftly to her side, and taking her hand in his pressed it to his lips, with a gesture that was as reverent as it was tender. For a moment something of the old brightness returned to her face as she bent her clear gaze upon his bowed head.

"You love me, Dan?" she murmured.

"You know I love you," he whispered passionately.

"Yes, I believe that you do," she said simply. "I shall always be thankful that I have won a good man's love." But suddenly she withdrew her hand, as the door of the bar opened. "See, here is Mademoiselle Nancy. She is coming for me:

she is to be with me to-night. There is much for me to do."

His heart surged within him; for he knew that in her simple words there was the tragic note of farewell; but he could not speak, he could not plead from that sad and broken woman for a passion that he knew but too well she could never give. He knew that she would leave him on the morrow, that his protests would be vain;—nay,— he would not even utter them! With the gathering of the darkness about the old Inn, he felt that the light in his heart was being obscured forever.

The evening passed, the night. Morning came, and Madame de la Fontaine, accompanied by Nancy, left the Inn at the Red Oak for Coventry. There remained to Dan of his brief and tragic passion but one letter, which Tom handed to him that morning, and which, with despairing heart, he read and re-read a hundred times.

"Mon cher ami:

"You would forgive that I do not know well how to express myself as I desire, if you could read my heart. I bade you good-bye to-night under the Red Oak, tree for me of such tragic and such beautiful memories. I could not say farewell otherwise, dear friend, nor could you. We have loved sincerely, have we not? We will remember that in days to come; you will remember it even in the happier days to come that I pray God to grant you. I know all that you would say, my friend, but it cannot be. I must vanish from your life, be gone as completely as though I had never entered it. I love you deeply, tenderly, but I could not be to you what I know that now you wish. All the past forbids. The very tragedy that proved to you that I was worthy of your trust forbids. It is my only justification that I saved your lives, dear friend; but oh how bitterly I ask pardon of God for what has been done! Then also, dearest friend, my heart is no longer capable to bear passion, but only to feel great tenderness. I could not say these things, and yet they must be written. I cannot go with them unsaid. Certain other things must be told you in justice to all.

"The story I told you on the schooner that day was largely truth. The General Pointelle, who was at the Inn at the Red Oak in 1814, was in reality the Maréchal de Boisdhyver, the father of your foster-sister Nancy. She is truly Eloise de Boisdhyver. The Maréchal returned to France to support the Emperor, as he wrote to madame your

good mother; and he fell, as I told you, on the
field of Waterloo. Admitting the importance of
his mission, admitting my ambiguous relation to
him (indefensible as it was), to have left the child
as he did was an act of kindness. In truth the
treasure concealed in the Oak Parlour is considerable, and it was always my purpose to return, but
the necessary directions for finding it were not en-
trusted to me, but to the Marquis Marie-Anne,
whom I didn't meet until many years after Waterloo. Then I was induced by the Marquis,—your
old Marquis—to provide the money for the miserable enterprise, of which we know the tragic result. From the first I was uncertain about the
method we adopted; and then soon after our ar-
rival here, from a hundred little indications, I became convinced that Bonhomme was prepared to
betray us, once we secured the treasure. As for
the Marquis, I suppose that he sailed away on the
schooner. You need fear him no longer. It was he,
I am convinced, that conveyed to them the information of the loosened casement in the Oak Parlour, and unwittingly arranged for his own undo-
ing and our salvation. At all events he will have
realized now that he has hopelessly lost the fight.
As for the treasure, by right it belongs to Eloise,
who should not disdain to use it. I enclose a

transcription of the other half of the torn scrap of paper, which will supplement the directions in your possession.

"And as for me, my friend, I shall seek a shelter in my own country apart from the world in which I have lived so to little purpose and for the most part so unhappily. Believe me, so it is best. My heart is too full for me to express all that I feel for you.

"Dear dear friend, do not render me the more unhappy to know that my brief friendship with you shall have harmed your life. Your place is in the world, to take part in the life of your own country, not, dear Dan, to waste youth and energy in the fruitless desolation of this beautiful Deal, not above all to grieve for a woman who was unworthy.

"I commend you to God, and I shall never forget you.

"CLAIRE DE LA FONTAINE."

It was with a heavy heart that Dan consented later in the morning to Tom's proposal that they force at last the secret of the Oak Parlour. He got the torn scrap of paper which he had found,— such ages ago it seemed, though it was scarcely a week,—in the old cabinet, and gave it to Tom,

with the copy of the other half which Madame de
la Fontaine had enclosed in her letter of farewell.
The copy in Madame de la Fontaine's handwriting did not dovetail exactly into the jagged edges
of the original portion, so that it was some time
before they could get it into position for reading.
But at last it was pasted together on a large bit
of cardboard, and Tom, with the aid of a dictionary, succeeded in making a translation, which Dan
took down.

"Learning of the attempt of my Emperor to regain his glorious throne, I leave these hospitable
shores to offer my sword to his cause. In case I
do not return, the person having instructions for
the discovery of this paper, which I tear in two
parts, will find herein the necessary directions for
the finding of my hidden treasure. This treasure,
bullion, jewels, and coins, is concealed in a secret
chamber in this Inn at the Red Oak. This secret
chamber will be entered from the Oak Parlour.
The hidden door is released by a spring beneath
the hand of the lady in the picture nearest the fireplace on the north side of the room. A panel
slides back revealing the entrance. Instructions
as to the deposition of the treasure will be found
in the golden casket therewith.

"FRANÇOIS DE BOISDHYVER."

"Well?" said Tom, "the instructions are definite enough. Now we can put them to the test. Let's get to work at once. Wait a second till I get some wood, and we'll make a fire in the Oak Parlour." He filled his arms with logs from the bin under the settle in the bar, while Dan got the key for the north wing.

Soon they were at the end of the old hall. It was with an effort that Dan brought himself to enter the room, for there flashed into his mind the vision of the last time he was there,—the cold silver moonlight, the dark burly form at the casement, the white drawn face of Claire de la Fontaine, and then the sharp flash and crack of the pistol.

But with an impatient gesture, as if to thrust aside these tragic memories, he stepped across the threshold, and kneeling at the hearth, took the wood from Tom's arms and began to lay a fire. In the meantime his friend fumbled at the window casements, opened them, and let in the light of day and the pure air of out-of-doors. Soon the fire was crackling cheerily on the great andirons and casting its bright reflection on the dark oak panelling of the walls. Nothing had been disturbed—the old cabinet with the lions' heads stood opposite the window; the little *escritoire*, behind which he had crouched on the fatal night, was pushed back against the wall; the chairs, the tables, thick with dust, stood just as they had been standing for many years.

"Do you realize, Tom," Dan said, as they stood side by side watching the blazing logs, "that it is sixteen years since General Pointelle stayed at the Inn and used this room?   And the treasure, if there is any treasure, has been mouldering here all that time."

"Let's get at it," said Tom.   "I confess this place gives me the creeps. Have you got my translation of the directions?"

"Yes, here it is."   Dan spread out the bit of paper on one of the tables.   " 'The hidden door is released by a spring beneath the hand of the lady in the picture nearest the fireplace on the north side of the room.'   Ah! that must be it—that old landscape let into the panel there."   He walked nearer and examined it closely.

It was a simple landscape, a garden in the foreground, forest and hills in the distance; and in the midst a lady in Eighteenth century costume caressing the head of a greyhound.   It was beautifully mellow in tone, and might well have been a production of Gainsborough, though the Frosts had preserved no such tradition.

Dan began to fumble, according to the directions, beneath the hand of the stately lady, pressing vigourously here and there with thumb and forefinger. "What's that?" he cried suddenly. A faint click, as of a spring in action, had sounded sharp in the stillness, but apparently with no other effect. "By Jove!" he exclaimed, "I believe there is something behind it. You heard the click? See there! the panel's opened a bit at the side." Surely enough, there was a long crack on the right— the length of the picture. "Here, let's push."

Careless of the landscape, they put their hands upon the panel and pressed with all their force to the left. It yielded slowly, slipping back sidewise into the wall, and revealed a narrow opening, beyond which was a little circular stairway, leading apparently to some chamber above.

"Here's the entrance to the secret chamber all right," Dan exclaimed. "Let's see where it goes to." He climbed in and started up the winding flight of stairs, Tom close behind him. About half way up the height of the Oak Parlour he came to a door. "Can't go any farther," he called to Tom.

"What's the matter?"

"There's a door here; it leads, evidently, into some little room between the Oak Parlour and the bedroom next. Who would ever have guessed it?"

"Can't you open the door; is it locked?"

Dan fumbled about till he found and turned the knob. "No," he answered. "I've opened it. But it's pitch dark inside. Get a candle."

He waited anxiously while Tom went below again to get a candle, a strange feeling of dread creeping over him now that at last he was about to penetrate the secret which had been of such tragic purport in his life. In a moment Tom had returned, a candle in either hand, one of which he handed to Dan, and together they entered the secret chamber. It was a little room scarcely six feet square, without light, and so far as they could see without ventilation. As they stood looking about the candle flickered strangely casting weird shadows over the walls. Suddenly they saw at their feet a tiny golden casket, and then, in a corner of the room a row of small cloth bags, several of which had been ripped open, so that a stream of golden coin flowed out upon the floor. Nearby stood another little golden chest; and Tom, lifting the lid, started back astonished. For there sparkling and glowing in the candle light as though they were living moving things, lay a heap of precious gems—diamonds, rubies, opals, sapphires, amethysts, that might have been the ransom of a princess.

"It's a treasure right enough!" cried Dan. "But what's this?" He turned to the opposite corner where there lay a heap of something covered with a great black cloth. They approached gingerly, and Dan stooped and picked up an edge of the covering. "It's a cloak," he exclaimed. Startled, he paused for a moment; then quickly pulled the cloak away, uncovering, to their horror, a lifeless body.

"Tom!" Dan cried in a ghastly whisper. "A man has died here."

Tom held the candle over the gruesome heap. "But who?" he asked in a hoarse whisper.

For reply Dan pointed significantly to the cloak which he had dropped on the floor.

"What!" cried Tom. "Good God! the old Marquis! But how? I don't understand—" he added, staring blankly.

"He must have come here the afternoon he pretended to leave the Inn, must have learned the secret passage somehow. It was he who loosened the casement in the Oak Parlour that night, and got his message to Bonhomme. He was waiting here for him. Can't you see it all—the panel slipped back; he couldn't open it again; Bonhomme didn't come; he was caught like a rat in a trap."

"My God, what a fate!"

"We can't leave his body here. We must give it decent burial, you and I, Tom, for we can't let this be known."

"And the treasure?"

"Ah! there was treasure, wasn't there? Wait, let's see what is in the little casket." He picked up the golden casket that they had stepped over as they entered, and raised the lid. A single scrap of paper was inside on the little velvet cushion, inscribed in the same handwriting as the paper of directions, *"Pour Eloise de Boisdhyver."*

"But come," Tom whispered, holding back the door, "I can't stand this any longer. We'll come back again, and do what must be done. Come, Dan."

Dan gave a last look into the strange horrible little room, then he followed his friend. They closed the door behind them and crept slowly down the narrow winding stairs to the Oak Parlour, leaving the treasure in the secret chamber and the Marquis guarding it in the silence and darkness of death. What had been so basely striven for was sorrily won at last.

THE END.

www.ingramcontent.com/pod-product-compliance
Lightning Source LLC
LaVergne TN
LVHW011941060326

832903LV00045B/120